THE GREAT DAYS AND SEASONS

THE GREAT DAYS AND SEASONS

Meditations for the Christian Year

BY LESLEY WILDER

Greenwich  Connecticut

1961

ACKNOWLEDGMENTS

Grateful acknowledgment is made to the following publishers for permission to use the copyrighted material from the titles listed:

The Atlantic Monthly—Antoine de Saint-Exupery, "Flight to Arras"; Anne Morrow Lindberg, "Broken Shell"

Dodd, Mead & Company—Elsa Barker, "The Vigil of Joseph"; Francis Thompson, "The Kingdom of God"

E. P. Dutton & Company—G. K. Chesterton; "The Donkey" in *The Wild Knight and Other Poems*

Harcourt, Brace, and World, Inc.—T. S. Eliot, "Little Gidding" from *Four Quartets* (copyright 1943); T. S. Eliot, *The Cocktail Party* (copyright 1950)

Harvard University Press—Theodore Spencer, *Poems 1940-1947* (Copyright 1944, 1948, by The President and Fellows of Harvard College.)

Holt, Rinehart and Winston, Inc.—Lizette Woodworth Reese, "Tears" in *Selected Poems of Lizette Woodworth Reese* (copyright 1926, 1954)

Alfred A. Knopf, Inc.—William Alexander Percy, *The Collected Poems of William Alexander Percy* (Copyright 1920, 1943, by Leroy Pratt Percy.)

Pantheon Press—Charles Péguy, *God Speaks*

Princeton University Press—Sören Kierkegaard, *Works of Love*

To the people of
THE CHURCH OF SAINT MATTHEW
whose devotion and love have contributed
so much to making this book possible

PREFACE

In Carson McCullers' play, *The Member of the Wedding*, there is a scene (III, 1) in which the negro cook, Berenice, is sitting in the kitchen speaking of the woes and troubles of life. In the room with her is the little white boy John Henry. He apparently has been sharing her feeling of sadness, for in his gentle, quiet way he picks up a large sea shell, holds it up to her ear and says, "You want to listen to the ocean?"

It would please me to think that these meditations might be something of a sea shell for those who have the patience and the charity to read them. Many of us, like the cook in the play, are so absorbed with the shallow and muddy waters of life that we fail to hear the sound of the ocean in the distance.

Those who try to interpret the great events and personalities of the Divine Drama of Redemption know that, like the sea, there is something unsearchable and inexhaustible about them. They move before us in ever changing aspects and moods—at one moment, quiet and serene; at another, awesome in their wrath. Obviously, in brief meditations one cannot do justice to these various moods. All that one can hope for is to convey certain undertones and overtones as one listens to the surge and flow of the sea, knowing that each one is only a faint echo of the vastness and the depth beyond.

I am assisted in my undertaking by the beauty of my surroundings. Very kind and generous friends have placed at my disposal their home, which is at the foot of Diamond Head in Honolulu. There is nothing between me and the ocean so that the first and last thing that I see and hear each day is the incredibly blue Pacific. Quite often a rainbow appears in the sky—God's messenger of reassurance and hope. I pray that something of that message may speak to you through these words which he permits me to say.

L. W.

CONTENTS

ADVENT SEASON

Advent is the great prologue to the drama of the Christian Year. It is the highway which leads to the sea. "Make straight in the desert a highway for our God." (*Is. 40:3*) The prophet and his spiritual successor, John the Baptist, leave no doubt in our minds as to what the highway is for. It is to be prepared for the arrival of God.

There should be no need to mention this point to Christian readers. But even among those of the holy fellowship, those who make up the household of God, there is a tendency to miss the real import of the Advent and Christmas seasons, due to involvement and concern with lesser things. Both the commercialism which precedes Christmas and obscures the solemn majesty and dignity of Advent, as well as the sentimentalism which brings tears to our eyes when we see the children with their presents and think of the Infant in the manger, tend to dull our awareness to the fact that it really is God we are preparing to receive and to salute on Christmas day.

With this in mind the pertinent question to ask during Advent is: What is the appropriate preparation and response when one is expecting a visit from God? Suppose we take our cue from him who was the great herald and messenger of the first Advent season—John the Baptist. Like the sound of a trumpet we hear his voice ringing out to the people of Israel, "Repent ye!" (*Matt. 3:2*) From this may we conclude that one appropriate response during this season is an act of repentance.

1

To understand the Christian concept of repentance one must first understand the Christian concept of sin, because sin is the thing we're supposed to repent of. In Mr. T. S. Eliot's play *The Cocktail Party,* when Celia tells her psychiatrist that she is suffering from a sense of sin, he asks her what she means; and this is her reply:

> "It's not the feeling of anything I've ever *done,*
> Which I might get away from, or of anything in me
> I could get rid of—but of emptiness, of failure
> Towards someone, or something, outside of myself." [1]

Sin is man's separation from God. It lies in man's desire to be separated from God. Sin is man's impulse to crowd God out of his life and to fill the vacancy with something other than God. No wonder Celia had a feeling of emptiness! Sin is not a matter of what we do but of what we are. For what we do is a by-product of what we are. The root of the matter lies in our hearts and in our wills crowding God out, preferring something less than God. That is why we hear more about Santa Claus at this time of year than we do about Christ. We prefer Santa Claus to Christ. Santa Claus is so pleasant and easy and friendly. He makes no demands upon us. We can go on living our shallow, selfish lives in the presence of Santa Claus and feel no twinge of conscience. There is no shadow of a Cross hovering over the figure of Santa Claus. Sin is preferring Santa Claus to Christ. "Repent ye, O my people."

A second response which is appropriate for Advent is suggested by the hymns appointed for this season. They all sound the note of hope and joy:

> Rejoice, rejoice believers!
> And let your light appear.
> *(The Hymnal, 1940,* #4)

and again,

> Hark! a thrilling voice is sounding;
> Christ is nigh, it seems to say. (#9)

Our attention is focused not so much on our sins as it is on our Saviour:

> Come, thou long expected Jesus,
> Born to set thy people free. (#1)

and again,

> Lo! he comes with clouds descending,
> Once for our salvation slain. (#5)

Advent, therefore, is a season of rejoicing. One reason for this is because the season brings with it the recollection of our Lord's birth in Bethlehem. There would, of course, be no Advent Season, nor any other Christian Season, if it had not been for that original birthday. We rejoice, therefore, because it is a time of happy memories. Think how empty and bare our lives would be if we did not have this capacity to remember—this gift of recollection!

Another reason for rejoicing during Advent is because the season means the continuation of our Lord's birth. It is a wonderful thing to remember the birthday in Bethlehem, and to ponder the implications of God coming into the world as he did in the person of the Christ Child. But that was a long time ago! What about the crazy, mixed-up world of today? What about you and me as far as the will of God is concerned? This is where the Advent hymns are so profound in their insight and wisdom. For in every case they are concerned, not with the past, but with the present and future:

> Wake, awake, for night is flying. (#3)

and again,

> The King shall come when morning dawns
> And light triumphant breaks. (#11)

In other words, the birth of God into our world and into our lives is a continuing thing. In a sense, the Incarnation at Bethlehem might be spoken of as a symbol of

3

God's constant willingness and desire to incarnate himself, to make himself available for the needs of his children. There is nothing local or limited about the activity of God. He is reaching out to you just as tenderly as the Infant Jesus reached up to caress the face of his mother. He is knocking at the door of your heart just as beseechingly as Joseph knocked at the door of the inn.

One final reason for rejoicing is the fact that this season promises the fulfillment of our Lord's birth. For during this season we are concerned not only with the first Christmas in Bethlehem and the continuing ones through the years, but also with the final Christmas when God will bring to pass the conclusion of his drama.

Every play has a final curtain, and God is much too good a dramatist not to schedule a final scene. The New Testament is filled with references to this scene.

> And I saw a new heaven and a new earth,
> For the first heaven and the first earth were passed away;
> And there was no more sea. . . .
> And there shall be no more death,
> neither sorrow nor crying,
> Neither shall there be any more pain:
> For the former things are passed away.   (*Rev. 21:1, 4*)

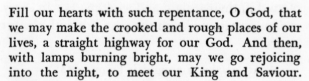

> Fill our hearts with such repentance, O God, that we may make the crooked and rough places of our lives, a straight highway for our God. And then, with lamps burning bright, may we go rejoicing into the night, to meet our King and Saviour. Alleluia!

THE CHRISTMAS STAR

It was not a very big star,
Its light was not very bright;
There were times of the year
    (when the moon was near)
That it almost faded from sight.

Its sphere on earth seemed quite dull,
No city great and fair;
'Twas only a village lay below
And an inn with a busy air.

The star had gazed so oft,
It all seemed a little stale;
'Twas always the same old country town
And the inn with the busy air.

Then late one night when the wind was cold,
And the ground was hard and bare;
The star beheld a man and maid
Enter a stable there.

The wind grew still and quiet,
The earth was like a tomb;
Creation seemed to hold its breath
Around that manger room.

The little star looked down
Into the Infant's eyes—
And from their light the star drew light
That brightened all the skies.

Angels hovered round,
Shimmering through the air;
Man and beast knelt down
And gazed in rapture there!

THE NATIVITY OF OUR LORD

Have you ever wondered why so few people seemed to be aware of what was taking place in the stable at Bethlehem? Have you ever thought it strange that there were so few visitors? The only record we have of anyone taking any notice of it at all is the reference to the group of shepherds and the three wise men. What about the crowded inn only a few yards away? Apparently its many guests knew nothing of this birth in the stable. What about the innkeeper, his family, his servants? Apparently they were too busy with other things. It is very significant, I think, that the only people we know of who took the time and the trouble to witness that scene in the stable were the few shepherds and the three wise men. What qualities did they possess which led them to the stable? Perhaps if we can learn that secret, we will know the secret of Christmas.

When we study the shepherds and the wise men the first quality we encounter is their simplicity. They were men who did not find it necessary to make a production of whatever they undertook. Therefore, the outward simplicity of the stable was not a stumbling block to them. They were interested in the person they had come to see, not in the size of his house or the make of his clothes. But more important than their outward simplicity was their inward simplicity. Most of us are so busy within ourselves, concocting schemes, making plans, fighting fears, that we simply haven't time to go to the stable. The crowded inn was full of these busy people. Only those find their way to the stable who choose *the way of simplicity*.

The second quality that impresses us when we study the shepherds and the wise men is their humility. I would define humility as being receptive to ideas that are different from one's own. I imagine that it must have been quite a shock to the shepherds and the wise men to see what they saw when they arrived at the stable. The shepherds had been taught that when the Messiah came, he would be a mighty deliverer who would make Israel a world power. The wise men were expecting to see the person who would be King of Israel. And here they behold two peasants with a small infant! It doesn't look much like a king or a deliverer to them. And yet, we are told that they bowed down before the Child. Here they are confronting a new and different concept of kingship, and because their minds and their hearts are receptive to things new and different, they are able to acknowledge him. Only those find their way to the stable who choose *the way of humility*.

A third quality that we notice in these men is their capacity to adore. Adoration is a word that we seldom use anymore, perhaps because so few of us adore! Adoration is a combination of love and worship, and it is something that we reserve for God. We are to love each other as we love ourselves, but we are to love God with all our heart, our mind, our soul. There is nothing partial or reserved or moderate or reasonable about adoration—it is giving of one's entire being. It is interesting, I think, that the only people present at the stable were the very poor and the very rich. And may I suggest that the reason why we do not even know the meaning of the word "adoration" is that we have made a god of mediocrity; and the price we pay when we serve that god is the loss of our capacity to adore. The god of mediocrity would be embarrassed at anything as extreme as adoration. Only those find their way to the stable who choose *the way of adoration*.

7

The final quality that we find in these men is their joy. If the shepherds had not been men of joy they would never have heard the song of the angels in the first place. You have to have at least a little joy inside you before you can encounter joy outside. If the wise men had not been men of joy (for joy is a by-product of hope), they would never have made that long journey following the star. The joy of Bethlehem is a joy that is not contingent upon the circumstances of life. Here they were in a cold, crude stable —Mary and her Child. There was pain and there was want. But there was also a deep, abiding joy, for God was in their midst; and where he is, there is joy. "Behold, I bring you good tidings of great joy!" Only those find their way to the stable who choose the *way of joy*.

Almighty God, our heavenly Father, thou hast shown the light of thy countenance in the face of our Lord Jesus Christ. Help us so to open our minds and our hearts to receive this light that our broken and crippled lives may be whole. This we ask in the name of him whose birth we celebrate this day, thy Son, Jesus Christ, our Lord. Amen.

A SHEPHERD'S SONG

Kneeling before the Christ Child

Soften your light, little Star!
Its radiance pierces my heart—
Revealing all things I have seen
Rehearsing all things I have done
Showing how far I have strayed
Telling the price I have paid—
Kindling a flame of desire
Warmed into life by your fire!

Close your bright eyes, little Lamb!
Their purity I cannot bear—
Calm and as clear as the night
Gentle and soft as the rain
Strong and as deep as the sea
Shielding a great mystery—
Heart without spot of stain
Lamb for all men to be slain!

Rest your fair head, little King!
Sleep on your dear mother's breast—
Dream of her sweet, lovely face
Not of your heavy, sharp crown—
Angels from heaven draw near
Sing lullabies in your ear—
Cherubim watch at your door
Wise men kneel down and adore!

SAINT STEPHEN, DEACON AND MARTYR

December 26

The scene has really changed very little since the death of Stephen. You will find the devil just as active and just as zealous for your soul as he was then. Only his weapons are different. Now they are much more subtle and dangerous! A good, clean stone you can see and feel and try to avoid. But the stones that will be hurled at you today are so very charming and soft that you will think it some sort of delightful game; you will detect no bruise at all until perhaps it is too late. They will be the stones of humanism, materialism, secularism; they will be the stones of charity—a little *c*—as opposed to Charity—capital *C*; they will be the stones of busyness, masquerading as godliness; they will be all those things that are the opposite of mystery, silence, and the supernatural.

In this meditation let us prepare for the stoning which is as inescapable as the Judgment of God. I can think of no better way of doing this than by referring to the stoning of Stephen and suggesting that we take our cue from him. We read in the Acts of the Apostles that "Stephen, being full of the Holy Ghost, looked up stedfastly into heaven." (*Acts 7:55*) In other words, he knew that what he needed more than anything else was a vision of God, so he looked in God's direction. The people in the Bible were so much better equipped than we are to cope with suffering and temptation because they were steeped in the theology of the Bible, which, of course, is a God-centered theology. Stephen had behind him the theology of the Psalmist who cried, "The Lord is my light and my salvation; whom then shall I fear?" (*Ps. 27:1*) Stephen looked up stedfastly into heaven. In other words, Stephen needed a God and he looked for a God who transcends the created order. Stephen knew that God uses the created order that we call the world, but when the world begins to go to pieces because of the sinfulness of man, then man must have a God who transcends the world. The Psalmist knew all this when he said, "I will lift up mine eyes unto the hills." (*Ps. 121:1*) Some may be surprised to learn that the next sentence, "from whence cometh my help" ends with a question mark, not a period. The Psalmist would never dream that his help would come from the hills, but rather from the God who made the hills. "My help cometh even from the Lord, who hath made heaven and earth." Stephen looked for a God who transcends "the whips and scorns of time." And because he looked stedfastly—not just now and then—we are told that he saw the glory of God.

But there was more to Stephen's vision than we have mentioned. He not only saw the glory of the transcendent God but he also saw our Lord standing on the right hand of God. "Behold, I see the heavens opened and the Son of man standing on the right hand of God." This is indeed biblical theology, for it includes both the old and the new testament. Therefore, in your vision of God will you earnestly search for some aspect of our Lord's countenance. For here is where the devil really concentrates. And if, through his subtle influence, he is able to confuse your vision of God, then he will indeed have something to be proud of. If he succeeds, for instance, in causing you to see some conflict between God's power and his love, some difference between God's justice and his mercy, that, of course, is exactly what he would like to do!

Stephen, "being full of the Holy Ghost, looked sted-fastly into heaven and saw the glory of God, and Jesus standing on the right hand of God." And they stoned Stephen. And he kneeled down and cried with a loud voice, "Lord, lay not this sin to their charge." He looked, he saw, he forgave. May I remind you that that is always the proper sequence. Vision must precede compassion, otherwise our compassion becomes charity—little *c*—not Christian Charity—capital *C*. And may I also say that this realm of compassion is another means of verifying the vision. For unless we are able to say of those who are stoning us, "Lay not this sin to their charge," then we can be sure that the devil is tampering with our communica-tion with God—that we do not have a clear, direct line and that our vision is something less than genuine.

Remind us, O God, that we must look before we can see. For that vision of thee without which man must perish, may we look toward that realm where thy will is supreme. Then beholding something of thy majesty, thy beauty, and thy love, may we reach out with compassionate hearts to forgive those who cast the stones. We ask this in the name of him who said, "Father, forgive them for they know not what they do." Amen.

SAINT JOHN, APOSTLE AND EVANGELIST

December 27

With many of the Apostles it is difficult to present any-thing in the way of an adequate portrait because of the very limited information about them. But in the case of St. John, we are given a particularly significant clue which provides a key to our understanding of him and puts him in a category all his own. For on more than one occasion in Holy Scripture, John is referred to as "the disciple whom Jesus loved."

We must pause for a moment to consider this rather startling descriptive phrase. Does it imply that our Lord did not love the other disciples or he loved them less than he did John? We cannot believe that he, whose whole life was devoted to proclaiming and revealing the universality and impartiality of God's love, would be capable of any-thing less than this himself. "He maketh his sun to rise on the evil and the good, and sendeth rain on the just and the unjust." (*Matt. 5:45*) I would not say that our Lord loved John any more than he loved the other disciples, but rather that he loved him in a different way. A father loves his children equally and impartially but he may enjoy the company of one particular child more than that of the others. Between himself and this child there exists a cer-tain bond, a closeness—a sympathetic understanding that is special and unique.

This was true, I believe, of the relationship that existed between our Lord and St. John. There was a David and Jonathan quality about it, one of those deep, beautiful friendships that is possible between men of great character and soul. That our Lord was capable of such a friendship is simply another indication of his full humanity.

Our concern in this meditation, however, is with what this friendship, this relationship, has to tell us about John himself. Usually, the closest friendships are between those who share the same ideals and aspirations—those who cherish the same values, those who are spiritual brothers. This being the case, we should expect to find in St. John, if not the same qualities that we find in our Lord, at least those qualities that our Lord cherished and enjoyed.

One of them, I feel sure, was a certain brightness of spirit, a great zest for life, that brought laughter and joy to those he met. The poet Wordsworth could easily have had St. John in mind when he wrote:

> The Soul that rises with us, our life's Star,
> Hath had elsewhere its setting,
> And cometh from afar:
> Not in entire forgetfulness,
> And not in utter nakedness,
> But trailing clouds of glory do we come
> From God, who is our home.
> *(Tintern Abbey)*

With most of us, the clouds of glory quickly fade away, but not with John. That heavenly aura rested as naturally about his head as the air he breathed, and shone as bright in Patmos as it did in Galilee. While scholars feel that John may not have written the Johannine literature in the New Testament, they do feel that he was the inspiration behind it. And what are the three great themes of that literature but life, light, and love? Because he was a creature of glory himself, John could write (referring to

14

our Lord), "And we beheld his glory, the glory of the only begotten of the Father, full of grace and truth." (*John 1:14*)

A second quality that we find in John is that of tenderness. But it is tenderness that proceeds not from softness or weakness but from strength. John had been a fisherman. His life had been a strenuous, out-of-doors one, and there is no reason to believe that he did not possess the sturdy physical attributes characteristic of that vocation. So when we see him at the Last Supper, leaning on the breast of the Master he loved, the scene is all the more moving because the tenderness expressed there is revealed through the power of strength. There is nothing in the world more beautiful than the gentleness and tenderness of a strong man!

We should not be surprised to find this quality in John because it was one of the chief qualities that we notice in our Lord. The Gospels are filled with examples of our Lord's tenderness—his treatment of the woman taken in adultery, the story of the Prodigal Son, the Good Samaritan—indeed, most of his ministry was devoted to caring for the broken, the crippled, the rejected. Therefore, we would expect that the person who was his dearest friend would reveal something of this same tenderness. They would have been strangers, otherwise.

But now let us come to the heart of the matter. For the first two qualities we have mentioned are really by-products of the third and primary one. The chief reason for the bond between our Lord and his favorite disciple is found in John's loving and lovable nature. Peter had to learn love through the things that he suffered. (This came too late to be of much comfort to our Lord during his earthly lifetime.) Paul had to learn love through conversion. But John had always loved. It was the essence of his being, and as natural to him as the laughter in his eyes and the joy in his heart. Of course, our Lord was drawn

15

to him as irresistibly as the sun is drawn to a mirror which is held up to catch its rays.

One final word before we leave this portrait. Will you direct your attention for a moment to the scene on Calvary's hill? There we see standing by the Cross of Jesus, in addition to his blessed mother, the disciple whom Jesus loved. There is no record that any of the other disciples were there. Was the reason for that their fear or guilt? Whatever the reason, we are glad that John was there. What a comfort his presence must have been to our Lord during those terrible hours!

We thank thee, O God, for John, the beloved disciple. May something of the brightness of his spirit, his tenderness, and the love with which he would lift the heavy burdens from the heart of his Lord, be rekindled in the Church of our day. May we be kind one to another, tenderhearted, forgiving one another, through Jesus Christ our Lord. Amen.

THE HOLY INNOCENTS

December 28

Psalm 73 is the portrait of a man wrestling with one of the deepest problems of human experience. We hear him uttering the same cries and asking the same questions that men have asked since the beginning of time. I dare say that there is no one who hasn't wrestled with this same problem at one time or another. It is the problem of trying to reconcile the concept of a loving and just God, with the cruelty and injustice that we see flourishing in the world. And on this day when we gaze in horror at the slaughter of the innocent children of Israel, we are confronted anew with this problem. In trying to cope with it we do well to return to the Old Testament and to the Psalms, where the air is so often filled with the cries of a persecuted people.

The Psalmist looks about him and says, "I see the ungodly in such prosperity. For they are in no peril of death; but are lusty and strong. They come in no misfortune like other folk; neither are they plagued like other men." (*Ps. 73:3-5*) If God is good and just and all powerful as we believe, why is it that evil so often enjoys the upper hand? Have you not asked this same question, perhaps more than once? And in searching for the answer I suspect that you have found yourself against the same stone wall that the Psalmist did when he said, "Then thought I to

understand this; but it was too hard for me." (*Ps. 73:16*)
Man has always found this problem too hard to understand. Job, you remember, that godly man whose suffering was so calamitous and out-of-proportion, kept crying
out to God, "Why? Why?" (*Job 3:23*) And even our Lord
could not refrain from asking, "Why hast thou forsaken
me?" (*Mk. 16:34*)

The Psalmist, however, was not content to remain at
the stone wall where his struggle with this problem had
led him. We see him moving away from the stone wall
and entering the doors of the Temple. "Then thought I
to understand this; but it was too hard for me, *until* I went
into the sanctuary of God; then understood I the end of
these men." (*Ps. 73:16-17*) What happened to the Psalmist
when he went into the Temple? What did he find there
that threw some light on the problem with which he had
been struggling? The answer to this question is a very
relevant one, for it points up what a true sanctuary of God
is supposed to be and to do. And as we consider this question perhaps we will gain a new insight into what the
Church is supposed to be and to do. What happens to us
when we enter the house of God? What do we find there
that the Psalmist found in the Temple which throws some
light on this deep problem of our souls?

For one thing, when we enter the church we are brought
into contact with eternity. The hymns that we sing, the
prayers that we say, the scripture that we read—all these
things have to do not only with the here and now, but
they also point to eternity. They are concerned with the
here and now, with the costumes and the scenery, the lines
which we speak, the roles that we play in this drama of
our earthly lives. But always there is the reminder that
this drama is fleeting and transitory, and our attention is
directed to that distant scene beyond "the heartache and
the thousand natural shocks that flesh is heir to!" This
glimpse of eternity does not solve the problem of the in-

justice and cruelty of the world, but it does lift us above the problem, and with the star dust of eternity in our eyes we are able to return to the problem with courage and hope. Without an occasional glimpse of that bright realm beyond the here and now it is no wonder that men's hearts are filled with despair. One thing the Church does is to bring us in touch with eternity.

Another thing it does, or should do, is to usher us into the presence of mystery. It speaks to one of the infinite and transcendent God. It reminds one of the frontiers of human understanding. It teaches one that no matter how far we progress in the realm of wisdom and understanding we still "see through a glass darkly." (*I Cor. 13:12*) We learn to accept the limitations of human understanding. We learn that there are some things beyond our understanding. The Church brings us in touch with mystery.

But unless the Church does more than this our worship will be a cold and frustrating experience. It is good to be brought into contact with eternity where our vision is extended beyond the shadows of the here and now. It is wonderful to be brought in touch with the mystery and to cry, "Holy, Holy, Holy!" But unless the Church also brings us into the presence of Love, we really are not helped very much with this problem of injustice. Unless we are able to find in the sanctuary of God some assurance that God cares, not only in some distant heavenly kingdom, but that he cares here and now, only then are we released from depression and despair. The symbol of our faith, the Cross, is one thing the Church holds up to remind us of the extent to which God cares here and now. The Holy Communion, or Lord's Supper, is another reminder. But unless we reflect something of this love in our daily lives, we are robbing the Church of one of its most convincing arguments as far as the love of God is concerned.

In the world there will always be sin, cruelty, and injustice. "Then thought I to understand this; but it was too hard for me until I went into the sanctuary of God."

We thank thee, O God, for the Church which was brought into being through the love of thy dear Son. When we enter its sacred walls may we feel ourselves in the Presence of Eternity, and find our vision lifted beyond the shadows of the moment. Help us to bow our heads before the mystery of the transcendent God that we may be willing to accept the limitations of human understanding. Above all, may we find in this place, and in the lives of our people, an expression of love which will help to redeem somewhat the cruelty and injustice of the world. We ask this in the name of Christ our Lord. Amen.

THE CIRCUMCISION OF CHRIST

January 1

Circumcision was one of the ancient rites of the Jewish people, one of the outward and visible signs of their faith. Our Lord, of course, was a member of that faith; he was a part of that tradition; he was careful to embrace the rites and the observances of his religion. But he knew how easy it is to remain in the realm of the outward and visible. He saw how many of his colleagues preferred to stay on the surface of religion rather than launch out into the deep; so throughout his ministry we see him pleading for the inwardness of things; we hear him appealing to the spirit of the law rather than to the letter. He was followed in this by his most zealous apostle. In Paul's letter to the Galatians we read, "For in Christ Jesus neither circumcision availeth anything, nor uncircumcision, but a new creature." (*Gal. 6:15*)

While it is true that the kingdom of God is outward as well as inward, that it is an objective cosmic event as well as an inner change in the hearts and wills of men, there is the need, from time to time, to give special emphasis not so much to "outward and visible signs" but rather to "inward and spiritual grace." In this meditation, therefore, we shall consider the importance of the inwardness of things.

21

Ever since the beginning of time there has been a tendency on the part of man to look for the answer to those things which trouble him most—not within himself, but outside himself. The fulfillment of his desires, the release from his fears, the meaning of his life, he has looked for not so much within his own heart as he has outside himself and away from himself. In other words, he directs his gaze not so much to the center but rather to the circumference —in a sense running away from himself, afraid to look within himself and ask such questions as "Who am I?" "What is the essence of my being?" "From whence did I come?" "Whither am I going?" Never troubling, really, to know ourselves! And if we do not know ourselves, how can we know our neighbors, our world, or our God?

Theodore Spencer presents the case very well, I think, in a poem of his in which he says:

> We are brought to this damnation, not by God,
> Not by blind evolution of cell to man,
> Not by the grabbing of money by envious thieves;
> We are brought to this damnation by ourselves,
> Trying always to live out of ourselves,
> Sharing too much, and not sharing enough.
> We try to live only in the obvious clamor. . . .[2]

It's time we began to look for our *selves*. "The kingdom of God is within you," (*Lk. 17:21*) Jesus said, and with words of fire he carried on his crusade for inwardness! "Woe unto you, scribes and Pharisees, hypocrites! for ye pay tithe of mint and anise and cummin, and have omitted the weightier matters of the law, judgment, mercy, and faith. . . . Ye blind guides, which strain at a gnat and swallow a camel. (*Matt. 23:23-24*) "Woe unto you, scribes and Pharisees, hypocrites! for ye are like unto whited sepulchres which indeed appear beautiful outward, but are within full of dead men's bones, and all uncleanness. Even so, ye also outwardly appear righteous unto men, but within ye are full of hypocrisy and iniquity." (*Matt. 23:27-28*)

One of the most profound treatments of this tendency on the part of man to externalize the problems of his spirit is seen in Herman Melville's great story, *Moby Dick*. This is not just another sea story about a man and a whale, as some think. It is a powerful treatment of the nature of man and the problem of evil. Ahab, the captain of the whaling vessel, devoted his life to searching for the white whale and destroying it. All the darkness and malice and evil that was in his own soul Ahab externalized into the whale. Instead of looking within himself and crying with the Psalmist, "Make me a clean heart, O God, and renew a right spirit within me" (*51:10*), he felt that the only way he could find peace for his tormented mind and spirit was in the destruction of the whale. The whale for him was the externalized symbol of the darkness of his own soul, and destroy it he must.

We all have our Moby Dick in one way or another— perhaps not as dramatically or as passionately as Ahab, but we too try to externalize the darkness of our souls. It is easier that way. We blame a whale or a bottle or a mother-in-law for the discontent of our own spirit. We try to externalize hell just as we try to externalize heaven, and as we fail, our Lord says to us: The kingdom of hell like the kingdom of heaven is within you.

It is a matter of inwardness! "Blessed are the pure in heart," Jesus said. (*Matt. 5:8*) They are the ones who see God—they are the ones who know what heaven is like. "Blessed are the poor in spirit." "Blessed are they which do hunger and thirst after righteousness." It is a matter of inwardness!

May we, who live so completely on the surface of life, always trying to externalize our heaven and our hell, heed the words of our blessed Lord and look within ourselves, making an honest attempt to know ourselves, our nature, our origin, and our destiny. "The kingdom of God is within you!"

O eternal God, who has taught us by thy holy Word that the kingdom of God is within us, and that our bodies are temples of thy Spirit, keep us, we most humbly beseech thee, temperate and holy in thought, word, and deed; that we, with all the pure in heart may see thee, and be made like unto thee in thy heavenly kingdom, through Jesus Christ our Lord. Amen.

THE EPIPHANY

January 6

In this meditation we turn to the Proper Preface for Epiphany, where we find these descriptive words in a reference to our Lord: "Who, in the substance of our mortal flesh, manifested forth his glory." We shall consider some of the implications of this statement.

First of all, we might turn our attention to the time which God chose for his work of salvation, considering the period of history which he selected in which to send his Son into the world. The first thing we notice about it is the fact that the time was not ideal. If one thinks that our own period of history is frightening, the same could be said of Palestine at the time that our Lord was born. The little Jewish nation was an occupied country—a tiny corner in the great empire of Rome. There was domination from without and revolt from within. Living there must have given one the feeling of walking on the brink of a volcano. It was not a time when there was peace on earth or good will among men. If God had waited for such an ideal time to do something about the world's salvation, we never would have known the life of Christ nor felt the power of his transforming love. If God had waited until mankind was rid of its selfishness, cruelty, and greed; if he had said: I will not send my Son into such a situation as that to receive such a fate as that—in other words, if he had waited for a happier time when his Son would have been received with open arms and acknowledged as King, then we still would be creatures without hope, having no light to point the way. There never is an ideal time!

There is a lesson for us in this Epiphany Preface, would we but heed it. There is so much that we could do to remove some of the debris in our lives, barriers we could tear down, shadows we could clear away, but we wait for a more favorable time. We say to ourselves, "Just as soon as I complete this big deal, or just as soon as I straighten out this domestic situation, then I'll do something about the heavy drinking which is getting heavier all the time, but right now I need it to keep going." There is so much we could do for the Church and for the kingdom of Christ, but we wait for a more favorable time. (The excuses that are offered when someone is asked to do a job!) The first thing that we notice about God's action in Christ is that the time was not ideal.

The second thing that we notice is that the material which God used was not perfect. "Who in the substance of our mortal flesh manifested forth his glory"—who in the weakness and frailty that flesh is heir to, the incompleteness of it, the temptations of it—who in the substance of this mortality, this fragility, this transiency, manifested forth his eternal glory. God didn't say: I must have a more perfect vessel than this, something that will transmit more adequately the vastness of my power and the glory of my love. Flesh and blood have such limitations; they are subject to things like diseases and pain and death. This is not a fitting instrument to manifest my glory.

The material which he chose was not perfect! And here we find the second lesson of our Preface. Some of us are not very attractive physically, some are not very keen mentally, some of us are not very inspiring spiritually, so that it never even occurs to us that we might be instruments for the manifestation of God's glory. We forget how beautiful imperfect things can be.

There is a lovely poem by Anne Morrow Lindberg, "Broken Shell," in which she considers the beauty of the broken fragments of shells that she finds along the shore.

> Cease searching for the perfect shell, the whole
> Inviolate form no tooth of time has cracked;
> The alabaster armor still intact
> From sand's erosion and the breaker's roll.
>
> What can we salvage from the ocean's strife
> More lovely than these skeletons that lie
> Like scattered flowers open to the sky,
> Yet not despoiled by their consent to life?
>
> The pattern on creation morning laid,
> By softened lip and hollow, unbetrayed;
> The gutted frame endures, a testament,
> Even in fragment, to that first intent.
>
> Look at this spiral, stripped to polished nerve
> Of growth. Erect a compass in its curve,
> It swings forever to the Absolute,
> Crying out beauty like a silver flute.[3]

The beauty of the broken shell! We forget that just as the North Star is all the more beautiful because of the darkness of the night which surrounds it, so is the grace of God all the more beautiful when it shines through some crippled body, some feeble or ugly frame. "Who in the substance of our mortal flesh manifested forth his glory."

If we were to choose a subtitle for Christmas and Epiphany, I would suggest this: "God, making the best of the situation." Choosing a time that was not ideal (no time is ever ideal), using a material that was not perfect (flesh and blood are never perfect), we see God making the best of the situation. And that is all he asks of us—to make the best of the situation in which we find ourselves, of a time that is not ideal, and a material that is not perfect.

There is one thing we usually overlook, however. When a man makes the best of a situation, both the man and the situation are changed. If he doesn't wait for some ideal time but takes positive and creative action in the time that he has, then his action will leave its imprint on the time and help to change the time; just as the action of God, during the confused time of Herod, changed all time thereafter. If a man doesn't wait for some perfect instrument but is willing to use a broken shell, then his act of grace and love will transform the broken shell and will shine forth all the more beautifully because of its very brokenness. "Who in the substance of our mortal flesh manifested forth his glory."

O God, who in the midst of a troubled time took steps in the direction of Peace; and using the frailty of human flesh, set out to redeem a lost world; help us to follow this godly example in trying to make the best of our own situation. We ask this in the name of Christ our Lord. Amen.

PRE-LENTEN SEASON

~~~~~~~~~~

We are told that following our Lord's Baptism he was led by the Spirit into the wilderness, where he spent forty days and nights in fasting and prayer. This was obviously one of the most important periods in his life. You might say that during those forty days the pattern of his vocation took the definite form that we see later in such bold relief on Calvary's hill. In a sense, the season of Lent, which we are anticipating in these pre-Lenten days, is an attempt on the part of Christian people to follow our Lord into the wilderness and to share with him something of that wilderness experience, in the hope that at the end of the forty days we may follow him perhaps a little more closely as he walks the painful steps to Calvary.

There were, no doubt, many different aspects in this experience but the Gospel mentions two as being especially significant. The first we shall consider now; the second on Ash Wednesday.

The record tells us that during those forty days and nights our Lord fasted. In other words, it was a period of rigorous physical discipline and self-denial. I'm afraid that the modern custom of giving up sweets and desserts for Lent makes something of a caricature of our Lord's discipline in the desert. Nevertheless, giving up candy is better than giving up nothing at all.

What was the point of our Lord's fasting in the wilderness? Was it because he didn't enjoy good food? Was it because he was so "spiritual minded," as we say, that he could get along without such things? Neither of these is the reason, for often we have seen him enjoying a dinner party with his friends. He was a young man and a healthy man—with all the physical appetites that other young men have. No, his fasting in the wilderness was a self-imposed discipline which he believed would help him to accomplish the thing he went into the wilderness to do. His purpose for going there was to learn what God wanted him to do with his life, and the way God wanted him to do it. This required such concentration of his mind and body and soul that he could not permit the distraction of physical indulgence. Recently I saw a number of children in the fields flying kites. They were able to get those kites in the air because the kites were light and graceful, and because they were fragile enough to be caught up by the breeze and buoyant enough to respond to the breeze. A man's body should be like a kite, stripped bare of clumsy excess, so that when God the Holy Spirit breathes upon him he can respond like a kite in the wind. Our Lord seemed to regard his body as a finely wrought instrument which, in the hands of God, could produce lovely music. He strove, therefore, to keep that instrument as sensitive and well-tuned as possible. That was one reason for his fasting.

Another was the nature of the combat in which he was engaged. I said a moment ago that our Lord went into the wilderness to learn God's will for him and his life. This meant that he was declaring a state of war. Our Lord knew that unless he could master his body, he could not hope to master his will. If he could not subdue his physical appetites, how could he ever control his spiritual appetites? He knew that disciplining his body could help him in the discipline of his mind and will. For these things are not unrelated to each other. Keeping our bodies in subjection has a very real bearing on keeping our will in subjection to God's will.

The chief reason, however, for our Lord's fasting was that this was just another way of exemplifying the motivating principle of his whole life—the principle of renunciation. Fasting was an outward and visible way of helping to keep alive in the world the flame of renunciation. Our Lord did not renounce things just for the sake of renouncing, but rather for the sake of his own and others' souls. And this matter of the welfare of souls is something we often overlook in our discipline. As Christians we are members one of another, and we have a responsibility to our weaker brethren. There are many physical pleasures that are perfectly valid and that may present no problem whatever to us. But if any of these pleasures is a stumbling block to some weaker brother, then renunciation of that pleasure on our part becomes a redemptive thing. It is lifted out of the realm of self-discipline and becomes an act of Christian love.

As we approach the days of Lent, will we walk with our Lord into the wilderness, along the pathway of discipline and self-denial, not just for our own salvation, but because of the help and strength it may give to a drowning man?

Lead us, O God, from the way of indulgence toward the bright flame of renunciation. May we strive to discipline our bodies which will assist us in the warfare with our rebellious hearts and wills. This we ask in the name of him, who for our sakes did fast and pray. Amen.

ASH WEDNESDAY

We have said that the season of Lent is an attempt on the part of Christian people to follow our Lord into the wilderness and to share with him those forty days and nights of fasting and prayer. In our last meditation we had something to say about the discipline and self-denial involved in that experience. Today we turn to the matter of temptation.

The Gospel puts it thus: "Then was Jesus led up of the Spirit into the wilderness to be tempted of the devil." (*Matt. 4:1*) This sounds as though one of the chief reasons for his going into the wilderness was in order that he might experience the great temptations which we know he encountered there. We said earlier that his main reason for going was to learn God's will about the nature of his vocation and ministry. Any man who has ever tried to do this knows how many wrestlings with the devil he must undergo, how much sifting of motive, how much purifying and surrender of will. Our Lord was no exception to this, and if he desired to run the full gamut of human experience, obviously this would mean not one but many struggles with temptation. It would appear then that temptation is a universal experience as far as human beings are concerned—that it is somehow included in the divine drama, and therefore a necessary part of man's spiritual pilgrimage. In the meditation today we shall try

32

to see what contribution temptation can make as we journey along the pathway to God.

There are perhaps a number of reasons why God included such a dangerous thing in his scheme for mankind, but before we discuss any of them we ought to consider some of the wrong reasons that are sometimes attributed to him. I am sure that in allowing temptation to play such a prominent part in the human drama God's purpose was not to test the strength of a person's character and will, as though God were a sort of cosmic athletic coach in charge of an earthly track meet, who would say to the runners: I'm going to make this race as difficult as I possibly can, filling it with hurdles and booby-traps. Perhaps a few of you may be strong enough and clever enough to get through to the end. There are people, you know, who think of God pretty much that way. Fortunately, our Lord did not think of him in that way; otherwise he could have never called him Father. If the purpose of temptation is simply to test the strength of our characters and our wills, then God is not a Father but a demon. He is not a shepherd but a wolf. For we have seen too many broken lives along the skid rows of the world, too many mere hulks of humanity whose characters and wills are not strong enough.

The purpose of temptation is redemptive—not destructive. And there are two ways in which temptation is especially redemptive. One is the way in which it joins our hands with our brothers! For there is no person who is not tempted in one way or another. There may be great distances between us as far as our virtues are concerned, but when it comes to temptation we are all members of one great brotherhood. The temptations may vary in their particular form or expression, but there is always present an underlying kinship. The person sitting on the one side of you may be struggling with great physical

33

temptations; the person on the other side with mental or spiritual ones. One of you may be coveting your neighbor's wife, and another your neighbor's bank account or social position. Some of you may not be aware of any particular temptation and, therefore, are in the most dangerous situation of all, like that of the man who said to me, "I never go to church but I live as good a life, if not better, than many who do"—completely unaware of the little figure sitting on his shoulder and whispering in his ear these subtle words of pride. When it comes to temptation, we are all members of the same family and, therefore, should reach out to each other with charity, forgiveness, and love. This is one purpose of temptation—to join our hands with the hands of our brothers!

The main purpose, however, is to put our hands into the hands of God. When God allowed Adam and Eve to be tempted in the Garden of Eden, his purpose was not to test them, but to draw them closer to himself. God knows how uneven the contest is between man and Satan. Man by himself is powerless in the hands of anything as demonic and subtle as the devil is. That was why God felt it necessary to enter the contest himself, and in and through his Son, not only to overcome the power of evil, but to provide the strength and the grace by means of which we too can say, "Get thee hence, Satan."

You may think that you do a pretty good job of fighting your temptations on your own without the benefit of God's help. This is a sure sign that you do not even know what your greatest temptations are! It is only when you put your hand into the hand of some frail brother, identifying yourself with him, and together putting both of your hands into the hands of God, admitting your mutual frailty and dependence—only then will the devil leave you and God's angels come and minister unto you.

O most Holy Spirit, give thy strength unto all who are tried by temptation. Help us to stand fast in thee, and make for us a way to escape, that we may be able to bear it; for the sake of Jesus Christ, our Lord and Saviour. Amen.

PALM SUNDAY

The story of Palm Sunday is the story of our Lord's entrance into the City of Jerusalem, and we call it the Triumphal Entry. It would hardly have been given such a title by the people who witnessed it so many centuries ago. As they watched that little procession coming into the city—a procession that was composed of nothing but a quiet, unarmed man riding on the back of a donkey, surrounded by a few followers who were singing songs and waving branches—they would hardly have described it as triumphant. Indeed, "pathetic" would probably have been the word they would have chosen, or even "ridiculous." There was no evidence of power, no signs of conquest, no indication that the rider had forced anyone to surrender, no outward display of glory. Wherein was the triumph that prompts us to call it a Triumphal Entry?

First of all, it was a triumph that was taking place within our Lord's own heart and soul—it was a triumph over self. All of our Lord's natural instincts must have cried out against that journey into Jerusalem. There he would encounter danger, opposition, criticism—very possibly defeat and death. All those instincts for safety, security, self-protection must have warned him against that entry. But somehow he felt convinced that Jerusalem was where God wanted him to be, and so we see him entering the city with an air of victory. There was something triumphant about that figure as he rode along on the back of the donkey. It was a triumph that had been won within his own heart, and one can never conceal the glory of those inward victories. They always show in the set of a man's shoulders, and in the way he holds his head.

In the second place, our Lord's entry into the city was a triumph over the situation. We spoke a moment ago of how almost pathetic, even ridiculous, that little procession was as it marched into the city with its palm branches and its songs. In a sense it was a caricature of a triumphal entry, and perhaps another man in the same situation might have appeared as a fool or a clown. But we see our Lord giving to this situation an air of majesty, a sense of grandeur. He takes what so easily could have been a farce and makes it a scene of triumph. Our Lord was master of the situation because he was first of all master of himself. It was because of so many previous victories over self that he was able to transform this travesty into a triumph.

So many of us allow the situations of life—the tragedies as well as the travesties—to master us, to shape us, and to mold us according to their own ridiculous or tragic themes. We become either a clown or a Hamlet, depending upon the situation. Our Lord's experience should have taught us that we can never be master of a situation until we have first learned to master ourselves. Our Lord's entry into Jerusalem was, first of all, a triumph over self. And because of that initial victory within, he was able to save the situation without. Our Lord never allowed himself to be the victim of circumstances. For even when he was nailed to the cross and stretched out for all the world to see, he was still master of the situation!

Finally, our Lord's entry into Jerusalem was a triumph for God. So often in this world the priorities are given to the world, the flesh, and the devil. Our Lord always gave the number one priority to God. "Not my will, O God, but thine be done." It was this God-centered priority that gave to our Lord that air of serenity, that quality of relaxed assurance, as he rode the donkey into Jerusalem. Our Lord was not tense about the situation of Jerusalem because Jerusalem was not his destination. God was his destination, and Jerusalem was significant only as a stop along the way. Most of us get so tense about Jerusalem because that's as far as we can see—that's as far as we want to go. Therefore, we approach the city anxiously, uneasily. But when we have our destination beyond Jerusalem, when we have God as our destination, then we can enter Jerusalem with a triumphant unconcern about what happens to us there. Our eyes are turned in the direction of another city, and our heart is pledged to serve another King.

Help us to see, O God, that we can never master a situation until we have first of all mastered ourselves, and that we can never master ourselves until we have learned to surrender ourselves to thy most holy will. Amen.

MONDAY BEFORE EASTER

In every drama there are always one or two leading players around whom most of the action of the drama revolves. But in addition to these stars of the play there are usually a number of minor characters that we refer to as the supporting cast. This was the case in the drama of the Passion. Our Lord himself was, of course, the central figure in the drama, but there were also other members of the cast.

Let us now turn our attention to three of the most obscure members. They are so very obscure, in fact, that we do not even know their names. But just as the drama of life is made up of many obscure players—people who are so much in the background that their brief appearance on the stage is seldom noticed at all—so was this true in the drama of our Lord's Passion. It is very easy to overlook the contribution which some of these bit players made to the total movement and impact of the drama, so that on this Monday in Holy Week, as we watch our Lord taking his place at the center of the stage to act out those final scenes of the drama, we shall look for a moment at some of the figures standing in the wings and try to learn something of their importance as far as the drama is concerned.

The first figure that we turn to is perhaps the lowest and the humblest in the entire cast. It is the figure of the donkey on whose back our Lord rode in making his Triumphant Entry. To me the donkey is a symbol, a representation of that whole realm of nature which played such an intimate part in the drama of Redemption. For when I think of the donkey I think of the whole created order of the Universe—of the star, for example, which led the Wise Men to the manger of Bethlehem, of the lilies of the field, and the fowls of the air that refreshed our Lord with their beauty and with their trust in the providence of God. I think of the sheep on the hillsides of Palestine, and our Lord's concern over a single one that was lost. I think of the donkey which possibly carried Mary to Bethlehem and which might very well have been present at our Lord's birth. How very appropriate that he should choose a donkey to carry him to his death! G. K. Chesterton has sensitively drawn our attention to this in his wonderful little poem "The Donkey":

When fishes flew and forests walked
    And figs grew upon thorn,
Some moment when the moon was blood
    Then surely I was born.

With monstrous head and sickening cry
    And ears like errant wings,
The devil's walking parody
    On all four-footed things.

The tattered outlaw of the earth,
    Of ancient crooked will;
Starve, scourge, deride me: I am dumb
    I keep my secret still.

Fools! For I also had my hour;
    One far, fierce hour and sweet:
There was a shout about my ears,
    And palms about my feet.[4]

The world of nature was much kinder and more responsive to its Lord and Master than was the human branch of his creation. The presence of the donkey in the drama of the Passion reminds us that the drama is a cosmic one.

It reminds us that the whole created order is involved. As the hymn puts it,

> Hosanna, our glad voices raise,
> Hosanna to our King!
> Should we forget our Saviour's praise,
> The stones themselves would sing.
> (*The Hymnal, 1940, #331*)

We turn now to another figure standing in the wings. It is the woman with the alabaster box of precious ointment. Palm Sunday is over. The week is moving on to its terrible and yet glorious climax. Our Lord is having supper with some friends at the home of Simon the leper in Bethany (*Mark 14:3*), which is in easy walking distance from Jerusalem. Suddenly a woman comes into the room (we are not told who she is), and she is carrying a jar of costly ointment, like some rare and very expensive perfume. Without any fuss whatever, without even saying anything, she pours the ointment on our Lord's head and the room is filled with its lovely fragrance.

It is difficult for me even to think of that scene without being moved to tears. How I wish I might have done what she did! Of all the characters in the Passion drama I believe that I admire and envy her the most. The insight and the love which she must have had! It was such a right thing to do, and it was such a right time to do it. Most of us are not so prompt in offering our gracious and sacrificial gifts. I think of this oftentimes when I see the expensive flowers at funerals. Too late! Too late! I am sure that as our Lord staggered under his cross on Friday, that the lingering traces of that ointment and the gracious heart which gave it must have been a source of comfort to him.

And there was one other actor whose name we do not know—the man in whose house the Last Supper was held. How indebted we are not only to this man in whose house

41

the Last Supper was held, but to all those men and women throughout the ages who have provided the material substance and fabric without which the Church could not carry on its sacramental life and ministry! The miracle of the Loaves and Fishes was a wonderful thing, but it would not have been possible if someone had not first provided the loaves and fishes.

Let us think, then, of those three figures during the days of this week, and the contribution which each made in the drama of the Passion: The donkey on whose back our Lord rode. The woman who lifted his heart with her sacrificial and timely gift. The man in whose house the Last Supper was held.

Help us, O God, to see that we are all participants in the drama of our Lord's Passion; and that whereas we might give him a helping hand from time to time, we also wound and pierce him in the side with our selfish and sinful lives. Lord, have mercy upon us! Christ, have mercy upon us! Lord, have mercy upon us!

TUESDAY BEFORE EASTER

On Ash Wednesday we noted that the Season of Lent **is** an attempt on the part of Christian people to follow our Lord into the wilderness and to share with him those forty days of fasting and prayer.

The Lenten Season, however, does not end with that experience in the wilderness, for today we find ourselves in the midst of a great city, surrounded by crowds of people. The central figure in the drama appears to be strangely detached from all the hustle and bustle that is going on around him. His eyes seem to be looking toward something beyond the immediate scene. And as we draw nearer, we find that it is the same figure we watched so closely during the days in the desert.

How long ago and far away that now seems—those days and nights under the stars! And what a contrast to the present scene! For instead of the silence and simplicity of the desert we are now confronted with the shouts of ambitious men, and all the rivalries and fears that go to make up the life of a great city. There are those who try to separate the wilderness from the city, as far as importance is concerned. To them the time in the wilderness is almost wasted time. They regard it as a time of inactivity—a time of dreams and prayers. The city, on the other hand, they regard as a place of reality. For a city is a busy place, a place of activity. It is filled with many people who are doing many things. Here, they say, is where the real issues in life are fought and decided.

In this, I believe, they are mistaken. It is true that the city of Jerusalem was the particular stage where the drama of the Triumphant Entry and the Crucifixion was acted out, but the place where that great drama was written—where the lines were decided and the central character found—was not in the city, but in the wilderness and during those hours on his knees in the garden. Christ's entry into Jerusalem on Palm Sunday, and his death on Good Friday were not the result of circumstances. They were the two great climaxes of a drama which, though conceived in heaven, was revealed to our Lord as he knelt alone in the desert and in the garden. Our purpose in this meditation is not to plead the case of the wilderness versus the city, but of the power of prayer and the vital role it plays in the destiny of mankind! For we can be sure that, more than anything else, it was our Lord's prayers that led him to Jerusalem on Sunday, and on Friday guided him to Calvary.

We ask, and rightly so, didn't his love have anything to do in shaping the course of that drama? It had everything to do with it! But where did his love come from? By what means was his love deepened and strengthened to the point that it could carry him as far as Calvary? Did that degree of love spring suddenly full-blown in his heart like Athena from the head of Zeus? Hardly, if the Gospels give us in any way an accurate picture of our Lord. His love grew deeper and richer because his prayers grew deeper and richer! That is one of the purposes of prayer —not to tell God a lot of things he already knows, not to ask him for a list of things which, if granted, might do more harm than good. One purpose of prayer is to draw close enough to God so that some of his love might brush off on us, and fill our hearts to the point where we will be able to join our Lord as he enters the crowded city— not because he likes the city more than the desert, but because the city is filled with God's children, and once you are touched by God's love you find that you begin to love what God loves! This way leads you into strange and difficult places. For God's love knows no boundaries, and if you walk with him he will ask you to help him as he stumbles with his cross to Calvary.

Deepen and enrich our prayers, we beseech thee, O God, by drawing us ever closer to thee. Deepen and enrich our love not only for thee but for all thy children. Keep us near thee in the desert, and in the city; through Jesus Christ our Lord. Amen.

WEDNESDAY BEFORE EASTER

The Cross is not so much a story of man's sin, as it is the story of God's love. And in this meditation we shall turn our attention to God the Father. Did he or did he not have a hand in his Son's death? Apparently he did—at least in the sense that he did allow it to happen. He did nothing to stop it or prevent it. He let Judas follow through with his terrible betrayal. He let Pilate wash his hands of the affair. He let the soldiers drive the last cruel nail. He did not intervene in any way.

Some of us as parents know how it feels to see our child in danger. Instinctively we reach out our hand to protect the child from danger in any form. Even knowing all the frailty and selfishness that is true of human love, we are convinced that we love our child. And yet we still have no idea of the depth of God's love for his Son. It could not have been easy for God to withhold his hand. There are two reasons, however, which may have prompted him to do so.

For one thing, most human parents are chiefly concerned with their child's immediate welfare. Things like food, shelter, clothing, a good environment, security, education, and a long life are given first importance. But God was chiefly concerned with his Son's eternal welfare, and he knew that in choosing the way of the Cross his Son was fulfilling his eternal destiny. How wise of God to allow his Son to be true to himself! Most parents would have tried to change their son's mind and have him choose some

46

vocation that would have been safer and more socially acceptable. But, you see, true love is only interested in the loved one's welfare, and a person's eternal welfare is much more important than his immediate welfare. God was refusing to do what many parents cannot resist doing, and that is to possess and control the soul of their son. "To thine own self be true," God was saying to his Son, "and though it breaks my heart I will not interfere with your eternal destiny."

God is aware that destiny and danger go together and that the higher the destiny the greater the danger. Remove the danger and you change and spoil the destiny. So few of us have any sense of destiny in this life. We concern ourselves with such trivial and immediate things that we shy away from any real danger; for real danger threatens our immediate welfare. Can we not, at least during this week, think a little more about our eternal welfare? What is our destiny as children of God?

Another reason why God withheld his hand is that he was thinking of more than just his own Son. St. Paul puts it in unforgettable language when he refers to God and says, "He that spared not his own Son, but delivered him up for us all." (*Rom. 8:32*) In other words, God realized that involved in his Son's death was the welfare of the whole world. And being the Father of the world and all its children, he did not have the right to protect his own child at the expense of all the other children. During the war there was no greater stigma than that attached to a parent who tried to pull strings either with the local draft board or with Washington, in order to land his son a safe assignment. We must expect God to have at least as high an ethical standard as our own. Had he intervened to spare his own Son, he would have been turning his back on the rest of the human race. But such is the integrity and unselfish love of God that he "spared not his own Son, but delivered him up for us all."

47

Yes, God did have a hand in his Son's death. He had the courage and the love to withhold his hand, and in so doing he allowed his Son to be true to himself, protecting thereby his eternal welfare and ours.

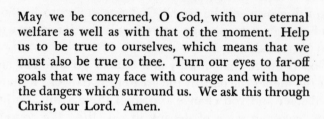

May we be concerned, O God, with our eternal welfare as well as with that of the moment. Help us to be true to ourselves, which means that we must also be true to thee. Turn our eyes to far-off goals that we may face with courage and with hope the dangers which surround us. We ask this through Christ, our Lord. Amen.

MAUNDY THURSDAY

We have considered man's part (but not his worst part) in the drama of our Lord's Passion. We have also considered God's part. In this meditation we shall consider the part which our Lord himself played in the drama. Was his role a passive or an active one? Did he go to the Cross as a sheep being led to the slaughter, blindly following where he was led, without any choice on his part, or did he have a hand in determining the scenes of that awesome drama? In other words, in going to Calvary was our Lord simply resigning himself to his fate, or was he actively and deliberately and voluntarily choosing his fate? This is an important point, it seems to me, for it will affect our whole attitude about the Crucifixion. If we think that he was simply resigning himself to his fate then we will regard him as a helpless victim of the proceedings and our response will be one of pity. But if we regard that scene on Calvary's hill as the climactic moment of a destiny which our Lord was freely choosing, then we will think of him not as a victim but as a victor and our response will be not pity but praise.

There is a line in St. John's Gospel which confirms this thought that the Cross was not an accident in time but a moment of destiny. Our Lord is thinking of some of the aspects of that terrible moment and he says, "Now is my soul troubled; and what shall I say? Father, save me from this hour: but for this cause came I unto this hour." (*John 12:27*) Our Lord knew that involved in these dreadful proceedings was not only his own destiny but that of the whole world, and he reached out with both hands to take the cup and drink it. In taking this cup, our Lord was not indiscriminately accepting another one of life's blows. Life is made up of many cups that are offered to us—some of them bitter, some sweet; and there are people who have a philosophy of living life to the full, drinking all the cups that life presents. Our Lord was much more selective than that. He believed in living life to the full, and no one has lived life more fully, but he understood that to mean living life in accordance with God's will. He knew that life offers us many cups that God would not want us to drink, and behind the radiance of the cup which he drank on Calvary we can see the shadow of a whole lifetime of rejected cups. He turned his back upon the three very attractive cups that were offered to him in the wilderness. There were also other very bitter cups which he refused. Once or twice before, an angry crowd had tried to kill him, and we are told that he slipped out of their midst and hid himself.

So if we take our Lord's life as an example, the key word for the Christian is not so much acceptance as it is selection. Some of the cups which life offers us we have no choice about—we simply have to accept them. But this was not true of the Cross. Our Lord selected that particular cup. Neither is it true of some of the crosses we feel called to bear. If, after we have been on our knees, as our Lord was in Gethsemane, in an effort to know God's will in the matter, we honestly feel that God does not want us to accept some particular cup, then we have the right to refuse it. But let us keep firmly in mind that whenever someone else's welfare was at stake, our Lord never refused that cup.

Will you think for a moment of the scene where Pilate sent for the cup in which to wash his hands—that symbol of irresponsibility, that sacrament of expediency. Then turn to the scene in the Upper Room, where our Lord reaches out to take the cup in his own hands, not to wash his hands of these very trying and unworthy disciples, but to fill the cup with his own blood which he knew in time would have the power to wash them clean and make them whole.

Someone once said to me that he felt the Holy Communion to be such a passive service. What a complete misunderstanding of its meaning! Let us see how very active and selective we are when we come forward to receive the Communion. In the first place, when we take the cup, we are not just taking a silver object filled with wine. We are taking the same cup about which our Lord prayed so agonizingly in the garden: "Father, if it be possible, let this cup pass from me." (*Matt. 26:39*) It behooves us to keep vividly in mind that scene in Gethsemane, that we may know the price which was paid for the cup we are about to drink, and the implications of our drinking it. Taking that cup cost our Lord his life. What does taking it cost us? For into that cup went not only our Lord's physical blood. (Anyone can sacrifice that!) Into the cup went his will and his desires, which he presented as a sacrificial offering to his heavenly Father. And when we take that cup, we identify ourselves with that sacrifice!

Help us, O God, to accept those things about which we have no choice or control. But when we are permitted a choice, may our selection be made in the same spirit that our Lord's was made in Gethsemane—"Not my will, O God, but thine be done." Amen.

51

GOOD FRIDAY

There is a glory about this day. We have reason for calling it good. Our Lord speaks to us from the Cross in words of forgiveness and love. But it is also a day of agony and darkness, and we tremble as we hear our Lord cry out, "My God! My God! Why hast thou forsaken me?"

This cry of anguish from the Cross is sometimes called the cry of desolation, the cry of doubt, the cry of dereliction. To me it is none of these things. I hear it as the anguished cry of love. The way we hear it, the way we interpret it, depends upon which word in the cry is emphasized. If we say, "My God! My God! *Why* hast thou forsaken me?" it becomes a cry of doubt, of questioning, of seeking for an answer; the cry becomes an intellectual one. *Why? Why?* If we say, "My God! My God! Why hast thou *forsaken* me?" it becomes a cry of desolation. The emphasis on the *why* questions God; the emphasis on the *forsaken* accuses God. "Why hast thou *forsaken* me?" When the emphasis is on the *why* it is our Lord's mind that is speaking. When the emphasis is on the *forsaken* it is our Lord's self that is speaking. In both cases our Lord becomes the center and the object of the cry. The cry is self-directed, self-centered: *Why? Why* am I *forsaken?*

As I hear our Lord utter this cry it seems to me the emphasis is not on the why or the forsaken but on the *thou.* Why hast *thou* forsaken me? Then it becomes not a cry of the mind or of the self, but a cry of the heart.

It becomes a cry of love. The object of the cry is not his own desolation but the God whom he loves. It is not self-directed but God-directed. He is not questioning God nor accusing God. It is a cry of anguish when he feels for a moment that he must have in some way displeased God and that God has turned his back upon him. The displeasure and the disapproval of man he can take, but not that of God. You see, we cannot understand this cry because we cannot understand the nature of our Lord's love for his heavenly Father. We who are so feeble in our loving, not only of God but of each other, cannot perceive the anguish that our Lord would feel in having God turn his back upon him.

You may remember the scene in John Steinbeck's book and film, *East of Eden,* in which the boy who loves his father so completely, and makes a supreme effort to offer him an expression of his love, finds that his father turns his back upon him. The cry of anguish that comes forth from the boy when his father rejects the gift of his love, when the boy throws his arm about his father's neck and the father remains cold and unyielding, is one of the most moving scenes I have ever known.

I am sure that the darkest and bitterest moment in a man's life is the feeling of being rejected by the person or the thing he loves most. Perhaps that is why it was necessary for our Lord to experience this moment of rejection. If he wanted to walk the full gamut of human experience, if he wanted to drink the same cup of man's tragic life in this world, then he could not be spared the darkest and bitterest experience of all. For there is nothing that equals it—neither physical pain nor death itself can bring the anguish that comes to a man when the person he loves more than life itself rejects the gift of his love.

The extent of a man's anguish is in direct proportion to the extent of his love. And one of the saddest aspects of modern life is that so few of us can suffer deeply because

53

so few of us can love greatly! There can be no real suffering apart from God. There can be pain and distress and misfortune. But all those qualities that make possible great suffering, as well as great love, qualities of depth and sensitivity and concern—they are all qualities that belong to God and we cannot know them or have them apart from him.

Let us not feel morbid or depressed when we confront our Lord's anguish. It is simply the reflection of his great love. And may we have the grace and the courage to deepen the quality of our love so that we might have what it takes to share at least a little of our Lord's anguish.

The tragedies of life are not what happens to people like Romeo and Juliet, and Socrates and Christ. The real tragedies are seen in the lives of people who are not willing to love greatly and who therefore cannot suffer greatly. The real tragedies are those who are spared the agony because they have never glimpsed the glory!

Steady us when we tremble, O Lord, before the anguish of the Cross. Then lift our eyes to behold its glory, the glory of a love in the presence of which we can only cry, Holy! Holy! Holy! Amen.

EASTER EVEN

It is appropriate, on this day, that we think of death. Our Lord has been placed in the tomb. The entrance has been sealed. The pain and the darkness of yesterday are over. Today there is the quietness and stillness of death.

It is sad, and a little pathetic, how hard we try to circumvent the thought of death. Instead of saying that someone died, we prefer to say that he passed on, or that he passed away. We no longer refer to death chambers— we call them slumber rooms! And the custom of banking the church and the coffin with flowers is an attempt, unconscious perhaps, to camouflage somewhat the fact that a person has died. It terrifies us to think that we, who "strut and fret our hour upon the stage," who pride ourselves on the way we can get along on our own, could suddenly be brought to such a helpless state, entirely dependent upon the mercy of God. Nothing could be more unchristian than the modern attitude and approach to death. I would like, therefore, to point out three things that go to make up a Christian concept of death.

The first is the fact that death is real. There is a poem by Longfellow that contains the line, "Life is real, life is earnest." The same may be said of death. Death is real. Death is earnest. And I suspect the reason why it is so hard for us to face the reality of death is because we have never learned to face the reality of life. Have you ever stopped to consider how very artificial our lives have become? There is a synthetic quality, not only in the fabrics we wear, but in our very souls—the layers and layers of masks that we wear in an attempt to hide our real selves. So that as a result, everything becomes artificial —our conversations, our relationships, our affections, even our religion! And the sad part is that we become so accustomed to things not being genuine that we are no longer shocked by artificiality; and we fail to realize how ludicrous it is, for instance, when we go to a graveside where, instead of the good, clean earth—the soil which has nourished us through the years—we find layers of artificial grass. One of the first things a Christian must face about death is the fact that it is real.

A second thing about it is the fact that it is necessary. Every mother knows this. Both the mother and the child must die to the pre-natal state—the state of the life in the womb—so that they might enjoy the post-natal state, the new life, and the new relationship which that state provides. Every artist knows this in the act of creation. He must learn to die to many things so that he might concentrate on the one important thing, for death is as necessary in the spiritual realm as it is in the physical realm. Our Lord had experienced many deaths and resurrections of the spirit before he was ready for the final one. Where there is no sense of the urgency of death, there is no sense of the urgency of life. Those people I know who are most truly alive are the ones who know that they haven't all the time in the world. Not that they dread death, neither are they obsessed by it, but they are aware of it—its reality and its urgency—and this gives to their lives a breathtaking quality with an insistence on putting first things first. If we do believe in eternal life, as we say in the Apostles' Creed, and if we do believe that death is the necessary gateway to that life, is it so unreasonable to expect that our lives should reveal some preparation for that great adventure?

Finally, may I say that death is the servant of God. If

the Easter message has one thing above all else to say to us it is this: God is the Master; death is his servant. So that in the Christian scheme of things there is never any question of who it is that has the final word. All things are in the hands of God—death as well as life. That is why Saint Paul was able to write to the Christians in Rome, "I am persuaded that neither death, nor life, nor angels, nor principalities, nor powers, nor things present, nor things to come, nor height, nor depth, nor any other creature shall be able to separate us from the love of God, which is in Christ Jesus our Lord." (*Rom. 8:38-39*)

And that is why our Lord was able to say with such confidence just before he breathed his last, "Father, into thy hands I commend my spirit."

~~~~~~

Grant, O Lord, that as we are baptized into the death of thy blessed Son, our Saviour Jesus Christ, so by continual mortifying our corrupt affections we may be buried with him; and that through the grave, and gate of death, we may pass to our joyful resurrection; for his merits, who died, and was buried, and rose again for us, the same thy Son Jesus Christ our Lord. Amen.

(*Book of Common Prayer*)

~~~

EASTER DAY

The great Festivals of the Christian Year are not only the commemorations of events which happened in the life of our Lord a long time ago, but they are also opportunities for the present and promises for the future. For example, when we celebrate Christmas each year we are not just remembering the birth of Christ in Bethlehem; but we are trying, at the same time, to make room in the inns of our lives in order that something of his grace and love might be born there. On Good Friday we do not just commemorate the sacrifice of Christ on Calvary, but we literally try to join him on his cross, and to nail there our own selfish wills and desires.

Likewise, on Easter we are not just celebrating the resurrection of Christ and saluting the empty tomb. We are also trying to expose the tombs which we have made of our own lives to the incandescent power of God, in order that we might roll away some of the stones which we have placed there. Easter is a day of hope for the present and for the future because Easter is strictly God's doing. At Christmas time God had the loving obedience and the willing assistance of the Virgin Mary. On Good Friday the fear and the evil and the complicity of sinful man was involved. But on Easter there was no one but God. Our Lord was dead, sealed in the tomb, and any possibility of his rising to life again rested entirely in God's hand.

In this age of humanism and of man-centered theology, it is good for us to be confronted with two great lessons that Easter has to teach us. One is the fact that God is able to do many things without any help from man. I was reminded of this during the nights of the past week as I would watch from my window the great golden moon, like some shimmering orb, begin its slow ascent across the sky. I am reminded of this each morning when the darkness in my room, like some errant school boy, grudgingly gives place to the brightness of the morning sun. I gaze at the beauty of the Pleiades and that bright cluster of stars somehow seems to keep its place and run its course without any help from me. I go for a walk beside the sea and the tides come and go independently of me. Easter reminds us of something that the Psalmist had learned a long time ago—that "God is our hope and our strength." (*Ps. 46:1*)

And now for the second great lesson that Easter has to teach us. This is even more important than the first, and the source of our greatest hope. God is able to accomplish his will in spite of the opposition of man. He does this not by overruling the wills of men and thereby trespassing upon the very thing which gives them their greatest dignity, namely, freedom of choice. No, he allows them to exercise their freedom in the fullest possible way, even though this means the death of his only Son, which it did. But God has a wonderful way of taking the misdeeds of men and transforming them into instruments of his holy will. God is unbelievably patient with us. He allows us to indulge our egos and our pride to an amazing degree. But when man begins to strut and to shout, "Look at me. I'm really quite a fellow. Why I can even frustrate and thwart the plans and purposes of God! I can even take his whole scheme of salvation and knock it into a cocked hat"—then we see the Sovereign Lord of the

Universe quietly extending his hand to bring his Son forth from the tomb, and to take that wretched cross and reshape it into a throne of victory.

Good Christian people, that is where our real hope lies—in a God who is going to accomplish his plan and his purpose, not just because of man, but even in spite of him.

***

> The Lord is King, be the people never so impatient; he sitteth between the Cherubim, be the earth never so unquiet.
> The Lord is great in Sion, and high above all people.
> They shall give thanks unto thy Name, which is great, wonderful, and holy.
> The King's power loveth judgment; thou hast prepared equity, thou hast executed judgment and righteousness in Jacob.
> O magnify the Lord our God, and fall down before his footstool; for he is holy. (*Ps. 99:1-5*)

THE GREAT FIFTY DAYS

This is the period between our Lord's Resurrection and the coming of the Holy Ghost at Pentecost. For the disciples it was perhaps the most difficult and painful time of all. The suffering and death on Calvary was at least something they could grasp—something that fell within the realm of their experience. They obviously did not understand the meaning or the reason behind it. They were astounded that the Messiah could come to such an end. Nevertheless, suffering and death were things with which they were familiar.

This could not be said, however, of their experience with the risen Christ. For here they were confronting not the natural world of time and space, but the supernatural world which is unaffected by things like closed rooms and locked doors. It is not surprising, therefore, that when Jesus suddenly appeared in their midst, "they were terrified and affrighted, and supposed that they had seen a spirit." (*Lk. 24:37*) We must remember the simple and rather earthy backgrounds from which most of these men had come. They were not a group of poets and mystics, but fishermen, tax collectors, and the like. Because of this, I have an idea that the period of fifty days following Easter was one in which the disciples experienced a great deal of bewilderment, uncertainty, and fear.

For one thing, it was a period in which the disciples were trying to adjust to change, and this is always difficult. In the first place, our Lord himself was changed.

Even his appearance was so different that when he joined the two disciples on the road to Emmaus they did not recognize him. (*Lk. 24:16*) But I suspect that the changed appearance was only an aspect of a deeper and profounder change which accounts, perhaps, for the first response of fear and awe. I have often felt that in those brief post-resurrection appearances, our Lord must have looked to his disciples very much as he looked to Peter, James, and John during the moment of Transfiguration on the mountain. There, you remember, "the fashion of his countenance was altered." There he was changed into a being of such radiance and glory that the disciples were dazzled at the brightness.

This change in our Lord's appearance and very being, meant, of course, a change in the relationship between him and the disciples. I have wondered sometimes how changed the relationship between Mary and Martha and their brother Lazarus must have been following his return from the grave. It could not possibly have been the same as it was before. Neither was it possible for the disciples to have the same relationship with the risen Christ that they had known with Jesus of Nazareth. Too much had happened to him and to them. His death and resurrection ushered them all into an entirely new dimension. He was no longer the familiar Rabbi and Master. Already they could sense about him the aura of the Lord of Creation. And we see them trying to adjust to the change.

We also see them trying to accept the loss. One of the reasons why this period was such a painful and nostalgic time was because it was a time for saying good-bye. "It is expedient for you that I go away." (*John 16:7*) And I suspect that no matter how much our Lord tried to relieve their sense of loss by references to the Comforter who would come—the Spirit of Truth—and by his promises that they would see him again, they still were shattered at the thought that something very wonderful and very beautiful was coming to an end. A particular chapter that was especially near and dear to them was drawing to a close. It was reassuring to know that there would be other chapters, but it wouldn't be the same.

The way we consent to our losses, the degree to which we are able to accept them, is one of the keys to the kingdom. There is in every loss, in every separation, some element of death. But what is true of the physical world is also true of the spiritual world. Where there is no death, there can be no life. "Except a corn of wheat fall into the ground and die, it abideth alone; but if it die, it bringeth forth much fruit." (*John 12:24*)

Surely there is nothing in life quite so hard for us as this matter of consenting to the losses of life, refusing to open our hands and let go of those things and those persons we love. We try to hold on to them just as Lot's wife tried to cling to the city that she loved and, in doing so, turned into a pillar of salt. When we look back and refuse to let go, life is bound to turn into a pillar of salt—something heavy, congealed, and hard. But when we accept the death of the past, and turn with eyes to the future, we find another key to the kingdom, and that is, that for everything God takes away, he gives something in return. Lizette Woodworth Reese points this up so beautifully in her poem "Tears":

When I consider Life and its few years—
A whisp of fog betwixt us and the sun;
A call to battle, and the battle done
Ere the last echo dies within our ears;
A rose choked in the grass; an hour of fears;
The gusts that past a darkening shore do beat;
The burst of music down an unlistening street—
I wonder at the idleness of tears.
Ye old, old dead, and ye of yesternight,
Chieftains, and bards, and keepers of the sheep,

By every cup of sorrow that you had,
Loose me from tears, and make me see aright
How each hath back what once he stayed to weep;
Homer his sight, David his little lad! [5]

O most loving Father, who willest us to give thanks
for all things, to dread nothing but the loss of thee,
and to cast all our care on thee, who carest for
us; Preserve us from faithless fears and worldly
anxieties, and grant that no clouds of this mortal
life may hide from us the light of that love which
is immortal, and which thou hast manifested unto
us in thy Son, Jesus Christ our Lord. Amen.

(Book of Common Prayer)

THE ASCENSION DAY

It was only fitting and right that he, "who for us men and for our salvation came down from heaven," having accomplished that which he had set out to do, should return to his throne in heaven where, as the Nicene Creed goes on to remind us, he "sitteth on the right hand of the Father." Let us, therefore, not think of the Ascension or of heaven in physical or geographical terms. Heaven means simply to be in the presence of the Father. The Ascension means to return to the Father's right hand —a distinction of equality and honor reserved for God the Son.

There are two implications of the Ascension with which we shall concern ourselves in this meditation. The first has to do with life here and now. We find our clue in the Epistle to the Hebrews where the writer is referring to the ascended Christ and speaks of him as the great high priest: "For we have not an high priest which cannot be touched with the feeling of our infirmities; but was in all points tempted like as we are." (*Heb. 4:15*)

In the wordly affairs of men, we know what a helpful thing it can be to have a friend at court. It is even more helpful when the friend is truly sympathetic with a particular need through having experienced that same need himself. He is able to intercede with the King in a much more convincing and persuasive way. Think, therefore, of the implications of having at the right hand of God a daily intercessor who was "in all points tempted like as we are." O lost and broken creatures of the earth, ye who feel crushed with the weight of your selfishness and sin, ye who tremble at the thought of a righteous and wrathful God, ye who are without hope, think, I beseech ye, of the great high priest sitting forever at the right hand of God and saying over and over again, "Father, forgive them."

The French poet, Charles Péguy, was aware of this aspect of the Ascension, which he expresses in a poem on the Lord's Prayer. In the poem it is God who is speaking, and he is meditating on the implications of the words "Our Father," with which his Son begins his famous prayer:

"Our Father who art in Heaven. Of course when a man begins like that.
When he says those three or four words to me.
When he begins by making those three or four words move ahead of him.
After that he can go on, he can tell me what he pleases.
Because, you understand, I am disarmed.
And my son knew it well.
My son who loved those men so very much.
Who had acquired a taste for them, and for the earth, and all that." [6]

We must remember that sitting forever at the right hand of God we have a great high priest, interceding in our behalf as he says again and again, "Father, Father."

The second implication we shall consider has to do with the life of the hereafter. We find our clue for this in St. John's Gospel. Our Lord is speaking: "In my Father's house are many mansions. . . . I go to prepare a place for you. . . . that where I am, there ye may be also." *(John 14:2-3)* Here we have the very heart of the Gospel —the Good News. Isn't it reassuring to know that there are *many* mansions—room perhaps even for you and me? There may even be room for those we feel certain are destined for the opposite direction!

66

As we said earlier, the Ascension was the return of our Lord to his heavenly throne; it was the appropriate benediction for God to make to his work of redemption. It was a thing complete and right in itself. But wouldn't you know that even this crowning moment of victory our Lord would somehow use for those he loved? "I go to prepare a place for you." It would be interesting, sometime, to count the number of times that our Lord used the words "for you." Even on the dark night of betrayal he could say, "This is my body which is given *for you*." (*Lk. 22:19*) If he could say such a thing at the moment of denial and death we should not be surprised to hear him say it at the moment of victory. "I go to prepare a place *for you*."

It is the last phrase, however, that brings us to the heart of the matter, "that where I am, there ye may be also." This brings us to the heart of the matter because it brings us to the heart of love. The lover desires always the presence of the beloved. "Having loved his own which were in the world, he loved them unto the end." (*John 13:1*) This, therefore, is the Christian's true joy as far as the hereafter is concerned. This is why, for the Christian, death is anticipated, not dreaded. For the one whose love surpasseth all things has promised that we will be with him. And, for the Christian, there could be no greater joy than this.

Grant, we beseech thee, Almighty God, that like as we do believe thy only-begotten son, our Lord Jesus Christ, to have ascended into the heavens; so we may also in heart and mind thither ascend, and with him continually dwell, who liveth and reigneth with thee and the Holy Ghost, one God, world without end. Amen.   (*Book of Common Prayer*)

PENTECOST

Commonly called Whitsunday

This is the day when we render special tribute to God the Holy Spirit, for it was on this day so many years ago that the Holy Spirit of God touched the lives of those first apostles, and transformed them from a group of frightened, bewildered men to men of power, conviction, and love.

There are several different symbols that are used to represent God the Holy Spirit, but the one I like best is the symbol of the tongues of fire. So that the title we might give to this meditation is "The Flame of the Spirit." Why is the Holy Spirit of God like a flame of fire?

Have you ever walked into a room on some dark, cold night, when the world outside seemed almost to cry out its feeling of loneliness and emptiness, and find inside the room a fire burning in the fireplace? Perhaps the first thing you think of when you see the fire is the brightness that it gives. The room is like an island of brightness in the midst of a dark sea, and you draw close to the fire so that something of its brightness will touch your own face.

So many faces that we see are filled with shadows—shadows of anxiety and grief. But seldom do we look into a pair of eyes that reflect any degree of radiance! We have to turn to our children to find this quality of brightness in their facial expressions, but often even their eyes seem dull, unresponsive, worried, and sad. There can be no true brightness of countenance except when our faces reflect the brightness of God, for it is the Holy Spirit of God, like the fire in the room, which is the source of all brightness, and we can reveal nothing of its radiance unless we draw near, and turn our faces in the direction of its wonderful light.

Another thing that strikes us when we leave the dark night and draw near to the fire in the room, is the warmth of the fire. And we stretch forth our cold hands and our cold hearts so that the flame of the fire may reach us with its warmth and drive away the chill which has made us numb and cold. The Holy Spirit of God is not an impersonal thing like the wind blowing through the trees! It is a very personal thing, because it is simply another name for the love of God in action. In the Nicene Creed, when we speak of the Holy Ghost or the Holy Spirit, we say, "*Who* proceedeth from the Father and the Son," and we mean by that that the Holy Spirit is the love which proceeds from God the Father and God the Son. And because the power of the Holy Spirit is the power of love, it is therefore a very warm and personal thing, and those of us whose hearts are empty and cold find, when we stretch forth our hands to the fire of God's love, not a cold wind brushing against our cheeks in the dark, not a ghostly and spooky thing, but a warm touch and a kiss from the flame which burns forever in the heart of God.

One final reason why fire is an appropriate symbol of the Holy Spirit is because fire burns. One cannot draw close to the Spirit of God without catching on fire, and this is the best test that I know of the reality and power of your spiritual life. To what extent are we on fire? To what extent is the flame of God's love burning us up as we respond to that love? Most of us insulate ourselves so carefully with layers and layers of protective covering, that the fire of God has very little chance of getting through, even to the outermost edges of our hearts. And when we find that he has succeeded in getting through, and starting a small flame in our hearts, we quickly grab the nearest thing that will extinguish it before we have time to do something reckless and rash—something with perhaps a bit of glory in it!

We all want the blessings and the benefits of the spiritual life without paying the cost. We want the love and joy and peace without getting burned, and we cannot have our joy and peace without burning. Where God is, there is the fire of God's love, and we cannot know that love until we draw close enough to catch on fire.

What a difference there is between the fire of heaven and the fire of hell! God's fire burns us but it does not destroy us—it is like the fire of the Burning Bush in which Moses beheld the Presence of God. The fire of hell is a frustrating fire, a destructive fire—there is no fulfillment about it. It is an awful and endless burning. The fire of heaven ignites us with its flame—yes, but heaven's fire creates, fulfills, makes whole. And the most important choice that man ever makes in this life is the choice between these two fires—the fire of heaven and the fire of hell.

T. S. Eliot expresses it very beautifully in these lines from *Four Quartets*:

> The dove descending breaks the air
> With flame of incandescent terror
> Of which the tongues declare
> The one discharge from sin and error.
> The only hope, or else despair
>   Lies in the choice of pyre or pyre—
>   To be redeemed from fire by fire.
>
> Who then devised the torment? Love.
> Love is the unfamiliar Name
> Behind the hands that wove
> The intolerable shirt of flame
> Which human power cannot remove.
>   We only live, only suspire
>   Consumed by either fire or fire.[7]

70

On this day when we pay tribute to the flame of God's love, we pray that we may choose the fire of heaven to save us from the fire of hell.

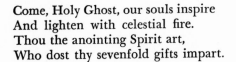

Come, Holy Ghost, our souls inspire
And lighten with celestial fire.
Thou the anointing Spirit art,
Who dost thy sevenfold gifts impart.

Thy blessed unction from above
Is comfort, life, and fire of love.
Enable with perpetual light,
The dulness of our blinded sight.

Anoint and cheer our soiled face
With the abundance of thy grace,
Keep far our foes, give peace at home,
Where thou art guide, no ill can come.

Teach us to know the Father, Son,
And thee, of both, to be but One,
That through the ages all along,
This may be our endless song:
    Praise to thy eternal merit,
    Father, Son, and Holy Spirit. Amen.

TRINITY SUNDAY

On this great day which we call Trinity Sunday, one of the words which we hear most frequently is the word "holy." One of the traditional hymns that we sing sounds the theme for the day. It is the familiar "Holy, Holy, Holy, Lord God Almighty." This is the day when we think of the holiness of God.

There may be a number of things which this word "holiness" will call to mind, but one aspect of its meaning, I believe, is found in the word "wholeness." The doctrine of the Trinity is an attempt on the part of the Church to recognize and to worship the wholeness of God's Being.

One of the things that gives to life its pathos and its tragedy is the brokenness and the incompleteness of human experience. Everything is partial, fragmentary, transitory, incomplete. As St. Paul says, "Now we see through a glass darkly" (*I Cor. 13:12*), and everything that we experience—truth, beauty, freedom, love—we experience, you might say, through a pair of dark glasses. In our brokenness and incompleteness we long for the wholeness of God, for we feel that the Psalmist was right when he turned to God and said, "Show the light of thy countenance and we shall be whole." (*Ps. 80:19*) The doctrine of the Trinity is the Church's way of saluting the wholeness of God. When we say God the Father, God the Son, and God the Holy Ghost we are trying in our feeble language to express the manifold richness of God's nature.

The nature of God shows us wherein true wholeness

lies, and those of us who long for a greater degree of wholeness than we now enjoy would do well to turn to God and, in the light of his countenance, find that which can make us whole. What are the elements which make up the wholeness of God?

We find the first element in the first person of the Blessed Trinity—God the Father, Creator of heaven and earth. It is the element of creativeness. There can be no wholeness where there is not some degree of creativeness. As a gifted young writer reminds us:

> If we are to draw our substance from a Whole greater than ourselves, receive our significance from it, we must first see that it exists. Man must give before he can receive, and build before he can inhabit. The gift to something greater than oneself is what my civilization called sacrifice. If I insist upon giving only to myself, I shall receive nothing. I shall be building nothing of which I am to form a part, and therefore I shall be nothing. And when, afterwards, you come to me and ask me to die for a cause, I shall refuse to die. My own cause commands me to live. Where is that rush of love that will compensate my death? Man dies for a home, not for walls and tables. Man dies for a Cathedral, not for stones. . . . There is a mystery here that is like the mystery of the infant's milk. The mother gives to the child. By her giving she creates her love. To create love, we must begin by sacrifice.[8]

Perhaps our lives seem as sterile and incomplete as they do because we have never paid the price of creating something. And as every artist would testify, there can be no creation without sacrifice.

The second element of wholeness we find in the second person of the Blessed Trinity—God the Son, Redeemer of the world. It is the element of redemption. It is quite true that on Calvary's hill our Lord offered a "full, perfect, and sufficient sacrifice, oblation and satisfaction for the sins of the whole world." And in that offering he accomplished the redemption of mankind. But we, as members of his Body, are called upon to be the agents and messengers of that redemption. And if our wholeness depends upon the extent to which we expose ourselves to the light of God's countenance, may we not forget that never has that countenance been revealed more radiantly than from the hard wood of the Cross, when with one hand he reached out to God and with the other to the whole human race, and he brought them together again, he made them at one again, on the bridge of his love. Most of us do not hesitate to reach out a hand to God, especially when we need his help. But we are too shy and reticent, or perhaps we do not care enough, to reach out with the other hand to some neighbor, or even to some member of our own family, to try to bring them a little closer to God. Therefore our Cross is incomplete and that is why our lives are incomplete. "Show the light of thy countenance and we shall be whole."

The third element we find in the third Person of the Blessed Trinity—God the Holy Ghost, sanctifier of the faithful. It is the element of sanctification. This is really an extension of the first two elements. For the word sanctification is simply a theological term which means "follow-through." Those who play golf know how important is the follow-through. It is not just the upward swing, not just the way one hits the ball, but what happens after one hits the ball that is important. The secret is in the follow-through. It wasn't enough for God to create the world and to redeem the world in the person of his blessed Son. There had to be a follow-through, and this we find in the strengthening and sustaining power of the Holy Ghost. This we find in the extension of our Lord's Body, the Church. The work of sanctification.

Many of us are able to create something because we are willing to pay the price, which is sacrifice. Many of us are able to redeem something through some act of generosity or love. But the follow-through, the sanctification, is where we are weak because that is often a tedious business, an unromantic, an unglamorous business, and perhaps the chief reason why our lives are not whole. We are willing to create a Church and we are willing to redeem a Church, but when it comes to the follow-through—that is when we have to get on our knees and pray for patience and strength and vision. "Show the light of thy countenance and we shall be whole."

Therefore with Angels and Archangels, and with all the company of heaven, we laud and magnify thy glorious Name; evermore praising thee, and saying,

Holy, Holy, Holy, Lord God of hosts, Heaven and earth are full of thy glory: Glory be to thee, O Lord Most High. (*Book of Common Prayer*)

SAINT ANDREW THE APOSTLE

November 30

Each year as we relive the drama of the Christian Year, I am more and more impressed with the insight and wisdom involved in arranging the Church calendar the way it is. For instance, the Feast of Christmas, which we celebrate on December 25th, is followed the very next day by the Feast of St. Stephen, who was the first Christian martyr. How wise of the Church, knowing that the Christian faith is very largely an antiphonal chorus between birth and death, to follow the feast of our Lord's birth immediately with the feast commemorating the death of the first Christian martyr—reminding us that we can never really separate Easter from Good Friday, that even over the manger in Bethlehem we can trace the shadowy outline of the Cross on Calvary's hill!

In a similar way we find real insight in the arrangement of the Feast of St. Andrew, coming as close as it does to the First Sunday in Advent. For there is a great central theme running through both these days, and it is the theme of urgency. In the Epistle for the First Sunday in Advent we read these words, "Now it is high time for us to awake out of sleep; for now is our salvation nearer than when we believed. The night is far spent; the day is at hand." (*Rom. 13:11-12*) On the Feast of Saint Andrew we read in the Collect that when our Lord called Andrew to be his disciple, Andrew "readily obeyed the calling and followed him without delay."

In the Gospel, when our Lord says to Peter and Andrew, "Follow me and I will make you fishers of men," we are told that "they straightway left their nets and followed him." (*Matt. 4:19-20*) All through the New Testament, and especially in the accounts of our Lord's life, we find this same breathtaking quality, this same sense of urgency. The time for living and loving, the time for responding to life and to God is not next week or next year, but *now. The time is now!*

One of the reasons why our Lord lived this way, and why he insisted on the same quality in his disciples, was that he was so sharply aware of the brevity of life. With the Psalmist, he knew that man's life is as a watch in the night, so soon it is over and gone. He knew that he did not have all the time in the world to find out and to fulfill God's will for him. And because of this consciousness of the brevity of life our Lord regarded each moment of time as a sacramental thing. He would have considered as a sacrilege the remark that people sometimes make, "Oh, I'm just killing time!"

This does not mean that our Lord was a busybody, scurrying around frantically to find something to keep him busy every single moment. As a matter of fact, with all the sense of urgency which dominated his life, he was never harassed or anxious or upset! In our Lord's eyes every second was sacramental because it was an outward and visible thing given to him by God to fill with inward and spiritual grace. So we see him making his whole life a chalice of love. And one thing we often overlook when we study our Lord's very active life, and marvel at how much he accomplished in such a short time, is the fact that for every moment of action there was a corresponding moment of prayer. There, of course, is where we find the secret of his serenity, and observe the great difference between his life and that of other active men, who so soon begin to show the signs of strain, because they show no signs of prayer.

77

The greatest cause, however, of our Lord's sense of urgency was not so much his awareness of the brevity of this earthly life, but rather his insight into the relation that exists between this life and the next. In other words, our Lord's attention was directed not only to the moments of time, but also to those of eternity, and he knew that the way we act out the drama of our earthly lives has a very real bearing on the drama of our heavenly lives. Death is only a very thin curtain between the two rooms of earth and heaven. Our Lord did not preach his Gospel of urgency because of the thought that this earthly life is the only chance we will get, and if we do not make the most of this life, we will miss out completely. On the contrary, it was his concern with eternity and the relation that exists between this life and the next that caused his Apostle to say, "Now is the day of salvation." (*II Cor. 6:2*) The time is now!

Will you try to keep these pictures in mind? One is the picture of the brevity of this earthly life. "The night is far spent; the day is at hand." The other is the picture of the very thin veil which separates this life from the next. The same soul that we die with we take through that veil. The third picture is that of Saint Andrew who, when he heard our Lord call to him, straightway left his fishing nets and followed him. The time for living and for loving, the time for responding to life and to God is now!

Give to our lives, O God, that sense of urgency which we see reflected in the life of thy Son. May we be so aware of the brevity of this earthly life, and of the thin veil between this world and the next, that each moment may be regarded as sacred and sacramental. This we ask through Jesus Christ our Lord. Amen.

SAINT THOMAS THE APOSTLE

December 21

According to the record, the chief thing that we know about St. Thomas (at least until the time of our Lord's ascension) was his capacity to doubt. There is, of course, a place in religion for honest doubt, for careful sifting, and for searching and weighing that which is claimed to be true. But unless the hesitancy of doubt is able to move on to some positive affirmation of faith then one is left in the limbo of shadow and indecision.

The temptation to doubt is a temptation we all share. Even our Lord seemed to be plagued by its subtlety; so that we might do well on this day when we think of "doubting Thomas," to consider this temptation and to ponder its effect on the life of the Spirit.

We shall turn first to the scene in the wilderness where we see our Lord struggling with this temptation. The devil says to our Lord, "If thou be the Son of God, command that these stones be made bread." And in the second temptation, when the devil refers to the pinnacle of the Temple he repeats the same phrase, "If thou be the Son of God, cast thyself down." Here we find the real temptation in each case—"If thou be the Son of God." It was the temptation our Lord felt to doubt his true nature and vocation as the Son of God.

What a terribly insidious thing doubt can be when we

are trying to be true to something! How tormenting it is to doubt the fidelity of your husband or your wife; to doubt the well-being of some loved one who may be facing an enemy gun or a surgeon's knife! Could anything be worse than to doubt the goodness and the love of God? The temptation to doubt is one of the devil's deadliest weapons. It assumes its most sinister form when he makes us doubt our true nature and vocation as sons of God. If he can succeed in doing this his battle is won. If he can somehow make us feel that there is nothing divine in our origin or our destiny, that there is nothing whatever to this talk of a Father-Son relationship as far as God and man are concerned, that man is a mere accident on the scene of life, no meaning or purpose to his existence, no hand of Providence to guide and sustain him, no heavenly Father to love and protect him—if the devil can just get that point across, the rest will be easy! This is a temptation that comes to all of us at one time or another, and I suspect that many of the things we regret the most, and would most like to forget, are things that have happened when we have yielded to the voice of doubt.

This same temptation came to our Lord to doubt that he was the Son of God. It was, in the first place, a temptation to doubt his true nature. But it was also a doubt as to his vocation. "If thou be the Son of God," the devil said. It was not spoken to an ordinary man to get him to question the fact that he was a child of God. It was spoken to the Incarnate One to make him doubt that he was the Son of God. In other words, the sense of mission and vocation which led our Lord into the wilderness in the first place, the devil was now trying to undermine by planting these seeds of doubt. How persistent the devil is! How he dwells over and over again on a single theme when he knows that man is vulnerable to that theme! From the beginning to the end of our Lord's ministry the devil haunted him with this temptation. Even on the Cross itself, you remember, the devil whispered in his ear, "If thou be the Son of God, come down from the Cross." You see, if he could get our Lord to doubt the genuineness of his vocation, the next step would be to get him to do something that was unworthy of that vocation. "If thou be the Son of God, command these stones to be made bread." "If thou be the Son of God, come down from the Cross."

The man who feels called to be a son of God in the special sense that a minister or priest is—what travail he must experience because of the devil's persistence in tempting him to doubt the reality of his vocation! And having listened to the voice of doubt regarding his vocation, how easy it is for him to do something that is unworthy of his vocation—making stones into bread for his own comfort; coming down from the Cross over and over again!

It is important, I think, to notice the times and circumstances under which the devil usually presents this temptation to doubt. Being forewarned is forearmed, they say. Notice that both in the wilderness and on the Cross our Lord had been through a very grueling experience. He was physically and spiritually exhausted. And it was just at that moment that the devil whispered his word of doubt—"If thou be the Son of God."

It will be the same with us when our moments of doubt come. It will be some dark, low period when we are ill or when someone we love is ill. It will be in the "valley of the shadow," when we lose someone who is very dear to us. It will be when the whips and scorns of time seem to conspire to break our heart and our spirit. All that one can say by way of comfort against the coming of such times is just to try to hang on until the fog lifts and the shadows flee away. They will, we know—they always do; but we must be patient and, above all, draw no conclusions during those dark days about ourselves, about life, or about God.

Of course, with some it may be just the opposite when the temptation comes to doubt his true nature and vocation as a child of God. It may occur when he is on the crest of the wave—healthy, wealthy, and wise in the eyes of the world. It may come to him some evening when he is sitting quietly before the fire. The devil may whisper in his ear, "Why bother about this business of being a child of God, with all the discipline and responsibility which that involves?" And when the tempter has planted this doubt in the man's mind, when he has the man seriously beginning to question whether he is a child of God or not, then it is so easy for him to persuade the man to do more and more things that are unworthy of a child of God. We never sell our birthright for a mess of pottage, as Esau did, unless the devil has caused us to question the beauty and the value of our birthright!

In concluding, let us recall what St. Peter said to the very first Christians. "My brethren, be sober, be vigilant, because your adversary, the devil, as a roaring lion, walketh about seeking whom he may devour—whom resist steadfast in the faith." (*I Pet. 5:8*)

Remind us, we beseech thee, O God, who we really are. Thou hast created us in thine own image. We are thy children and heirs of eternal life. With this as our true nature and vocation, assist us as we struggle with those temptations which would hide from us the beauty of our sonship. This we ask in the name of him of whom thou didst say, "This is my beloved Son in whom I am well pleased." Amen.

THE CONVERSION OF SAINT PAUL

January 25

The conversion of St. Paul is one of the great and dramatic religious experiences of all time. Is there anyone who is not familiar with that scene on the Damascus Road, when the zealous young Pharisee Saul, doing his best to stamp out this new religion marching under the banner of Jesus Christ, was suddenly thrown to the ground by the impact of a shining light from heaven and a voice cried to him, "Saul, Saul, why persecutest thou me?" (*Acts 9:4*) The scene is electric in its power, and every time we think of the conversion of St. Paul we think of that scene on the Damascus Road.

Perhaps that is why there is such confusion and misunderstanding about the meaning of the term conversion. We are not familiar, in our own experience, with the kind of thing that happened on the Damascus Road. The changes and the conversion in people's lives that we know have not happened that way. But just because we do not see shining lights, nor hear voices, does not mean that conversion does not take place. I have seen too many people, whose lives like that of Saul (using the wrong means to arrive at the wrong ends), become completely redirected in both ends and means so that what you have is literally a new person. To me, the important thing about conversion is not so much the dramatic and climactic moment when, after a long period of darkness, one suddenly sees a flame of light, but all the things that lead up to that moment which make the moment possible, and the things which follow the moment that reveal its genuineness and truth. So, in thinking about St. Paul's conversion from one of the greatest enemies of Christ to one of his bravest soldiers, a conversion that went so deep that it changed his very name, we shall consider not the scene on the Damascus Road, but two other scenes—one which happened before the Damascus Road experience, and the other which happened after.

The first is the stoning of Stephen. In our meditation on St. Stephen we mention the very beautiful way in which he met his death, interceding with God on behalf of those who were stoning him. "Lord, lay not this sin to their charge." (*Acts 7:60*) We mention this account of Stephen's death because we are told that the witnesses who stoned him "laid down their clothes at a young man's feet whose name was Saul." (*Acts 7:58*) What thoughts went through Saul's mind as he watched Stephen die? How was Saul, so sensitive and so intense, affected by the spirit which Stephen revealed as he met his death? For a long time I have felt that the way Stephen died was one of the strongest factors leading to Saul's conversion—one of the chief things which prepared his mind and his heart for the experience on the Damascus Road. We never realize the extent of our influence, how some word that we say, some kindness that we offer, some bravery that we show, some love that we extend, might be the thing which marks the turning point in a person's life, setting in motion forces which, with God's help, gradually produce a new soul, a new life.

The next scene takes place several years after Paul's conversion. He is a prisoner on his way to Rome to be tried by Caesar. Before he is sent to Rome he is brought before King Agrippa and proceeds to tell his story. He describes to the king his experience on the Damascus

Road and he concludes with the words, "Whereupon, O King Agrippa, I was not disobedient unto the heavenly vision." Here we see the real test of the genuineness of his conversion. What difference did it make in his life? How long did his conversion last? How stedfast was the effect of that shining hour on the way to Damascus? "Whereupon, O King Agrippa, I was not disobedient unto the heavenly vision." And when we see the figure of Paul, like a flaming sword, burning the sign of the Cross into the whole region of the Mediterranean world, we realize how deep and how true his conversion really was. If we are alert and sensitive as Paul was to the action of God in every experience, then we will see, as he did, in the stonings and tragedies of life, the love of God revealing itself. This will be like leaven at work in our souls until, at last, when perhaps we least expect it, we too will have our shining moment as we journey on the Damascus Road. It may be a very quiet and simple moment—no light and no voices—but it will be real and we will know that it is real! Afterward will come the testing time when in patient and stedfast devotion to the call which God has given us, we will endeavor not to be disobedient unto the heavenly vision.

We thank thee, O God, for the reminder which is given us in the life of St. Paul, that it is never too late to change. Keep us sensitive to the workings of the Holy Spirit in all areas of life. Then, having seen the vision, may we be stedfast and obedient. This we ask through Jesus Christ our Lord. Amen.

THE PRESENTATION OF CHRIST
IN THE TEMPLE

February 2

This is one of the great and beautiful feast days of the Church Year—the Presentation of Christ in the Temple, commonly called The Purification of Saint Mary the Virgin. There was an ancient Jewish law which required that every male child shall be called holy, and that shortly after his birth the mother shall bring the child to the Temple to dedicate him to God, and to make a sacrificial offering of a pair of turtle doves or two young pigeons.

Mary and Joseph did not regard lightly the religious laws and observances of their people. As we read in St. Luke's Gospel, "When the days of her purification according to the law of Moses were accomplished they brought him [the child Jesus] to Jerusalem to present him to the Lord . . . and to offer a sacrifice according to that which is said in the law of the Lord, a pair of turtle doves, or two young pigeons." (*Lk. 2:22-24*) To me this is one of the most beautiful and one of the tenderest scenes in the New Testament—this scene in the Temple, of Mary and Joseph, observing so carefully the religious laws of their people, coming to present their child to God and to make their sacrificial offering.

We would do well to gaze at that scene with great care, and with the hope that something of its simplicity and grace might be imprinted within our own hearts, for we live in an age that is quite indifferent to the outward and visible observances of our faith. Our religion has become so very subjective, so very introverted, that we believe the only important thing is how we feel within ourselves. Naturally, we would not want the outward and visible observances to become a substitute for inward and spiritual grace, but the Church has always believed—and apparently Mary and Joseph, together with our Lord, shared this belief—that the outward and visible observances play a very real part in the cultivation of inward and spiritual grace. This, indeed, is the very basis of the sacramental principle on which our faith is founded. We see this principle in action not only in the realm of religion, but also in the realm of just plain, everyday manners. I am certain that the reason why we witness so little courtesy, so little dignity anymore, is because we have grown so careless in our observance of outward and visible things.

When I was a boy I never fully understood why my father insisted that in answering him or my mother, I should always say "Yes, sir" or "No, sir," "Yes, ma'am" or "No, ma'am," and there were times, I am sure, when I rebelled against this formality. Now I realize how indebted I am to them for that teaching, for I am able to see how much the commandment—"Honor thy father and thy mother"—was made more meaningful and effective by the observance of this formality. My parents and I were always great friends, but there was never the buddy-buddy kind of relationship that is so popular today; and I wonder oftentimes if our parents do their children a favor in permitting a relationship that does not insist upon some degree of formality. A boy and a girl need in their parents, not someone who is a buddy, but someone who is a father and a mother!

In the Temple scene where Mary and Joseph stand by

the priest, holding the child Jesus and offering their sacrifice, there is something very simple and natural—something wonderfully objective. They did not perform this act because they thought it would make them feel good inside. I am sure that both Mary and Joseph would have been shocked if someone had suggested to them that the reality and the validity of this act of worship depended upon whether or not it gave them a nice, warm feeling. They obviously would not remain unmoved by an act of worship so beautiful and meaningful, but that is not why they did it. They were simply fulfilling the religious observances of their faith, something which completely transcended their own feeling or convenience in the matter.

We could use a little of this objectivity in the observance of our religion. Believe me, there is a special blessing that it gives! It is the kind of blessing that came to the aged Simeon, who was present in the Temple when Mary and Joseph brought in the Child Jesus. Simeon was a very old man. For many, many years he had faithfully fulfilled the religious observances of his faith. There were no doubt times, now and then, when he felt a certain glow inside. But I suspect that most of the time it was simply the quiet fulfillment of a duty, with all the dryness and all the dullness that usually goes with duty. But to him who perseveres unto the end there is vouchsafed a special blessing; for after all the years of waiting and worshipping in the Temple, Simeon was given the insight to recognize the Lord Christ when he appeared. There must have been many people in Jerusalem that day when Mary and Joseph came in. But as far as we know, only two recognized our Lord—Simeon and the prophetess Anna. Could there be some relation between their presence in the Temple, quietly fulfilling their duty, and their insight which came as a benediction? Simeon took the Child in his arms and said:

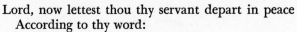

Lord, now lettest thou thy servant depart in peace
  According to thy word:
For mine eyes have seen thy salvation,
  Which thou hast prepared before the face of all
    people;
A light to lighten the Gentiles,
  And the glory of thy people Israel.

(Lk. 2:29-32)

SAINT MATTHIAS THE APOSTLE

February 24

The choice of Matthias to fill the place caused by the betrayal and death of Judas points up certain truths about man and God that we would do well to consider. The story, of course, is as old as the story of man himself—the loss of one individual through failure, death, or defeat; the choice of another to fill his place.

The first lesson we might learn from this is the fact that no one is indispensable. There are an amazing number of people in the world who have an exaggerated sense of their own importance and who take themselves much too seriously. This is especially apparent in the world of business. Look at the tense and harassed expression on the faces of many of the executives that you meet (especially the ones who are "on the way up"). The weight of the universe appears to rest on their shoulders and they act as though a mistake or failure on their part would mean the end of everything.

This is not said to suggest that a man should take his responsibilities lightly. Judas's failure to himself and to his Lord was something so terrible and so costly that even today we shudder at the thought of it. But wasn't his pride and feeling of self-importance really the cause of it all? Wasn't the fact that he presumed to be the best judge of the situation, as far as our Lord was concerned, the very thing which caused him to force the issue? Was it perhaps that he held a different concept of the Messiah in his mind and began to question our Lord's genuineness? Judas took himself too seriously. He began to think of himself as indispensable to God's scheme of salvation!

The second lesson that the story suggests to us is this: God's truth goes marching on. The Prophet Isaiah had learned this lesson centuries before, when he heard God say:

> For as the rain cometh down, and the snow from heaven, and returneth not thither, but watereth the earth, and maketh it bring forth and bud, that it may give seed to the sower, and bread to the eater:
> So shall my word be that goeth forth out of the mouth: it shall not return unto me void, but it shall prosper in the thing whereto I sent it. (*Is. 55:10-11*)

There have been many failures and defeats that God has had to cope with ever since Eve (and Adam) succumbed to the charm of the forbidden fruit. But we do not see God giving up in despair. Over and over again throughout the ages we see him choosing some new Matthias to fill the place of another Judas. The Matthias he chooses does not do the job the same way that Judas would have done—perhaps not nearly as well—but this is not important. The important thing is that the work goes on! God's word does not return to him void.

> Though the cause of evil prosper,
>   Yet 'tis truth alone is strong:
> Though her portion be the scaffold,
>   And upon the throne be wrong,
> Yet that scaffold sways the future,
>   And, behind the dim unknown,
> Standeth God within the shadow,
>   Keeping watch above his own.
>   (*The Hymnal, 1940, #519*)

But there is one final lesson we learn from the choice of Matthias. It is this: the Holy Spirit does respond to

91

appeals for guidance and help. I know that we often question this, even in the life and government of the Church. Like Judas, we feel that our concept, or our man, would be much the better choice. And while we cannot deny that sinful man is able to act contrary to the wisdom and will of the Holy Spirit, we must affirm that it is better to run that risk than to close the door to democratic procedure.

The choice of Matthias was the choice of the group. Lots were cast to determine which of the two men—Justus or Matthias—would be chosen. "And they prayed, and said, 'Thou, Lord, which knowest the hearts of all men, shew whether of these two thou hast chosen.' . . . And they gave forth their lots; and the lot fell upon Matthias." (*Acts 1:24,26*)

There were, no doubt, elements of human frailty involved in the choice, personal affections and animosities. But when a group of sincere and devout men ask for guidance from the Holy Spirit, he does not turn his back upon them. Either choice may have been far from ideal, but if the one chosen was the lesser of two evils, then the choice was the right choice; for this is often the only choice vouchsafed to us in this naughty world.

Give us a true perspective, O God, that we may not take ourselves too seriously. Remind us that there are others upon whom thou canst call for the work which has to be done. Then may we trust that what thou desirest to be done will be done, in thine own time and way; through Jesus Christ our Lord. Amen.

THE ANNUNCIATION OF THE BLESSED VIRGIN MARY

March 25

The angelic messenger announced to Mary, "Behold, thou shalt conceive in thy womb, and bring forth a son, and shalt call his name Jesus. He shall be great and shall be called the Son of the Highest." (*Lk. 1:31-32*) Thus did God call Mary to her very special and wonderful vocation. In this meditation we shall consider the nature of her response.

It is quite apparent that her first response was one of fear. We are told that when she saw the angel and heard his greeting, "she was troubled at his saying, and cast in her mind what manner of salutation this should be. And the angel said unto her, 'Fear not, Mary.'" It is not surprising that she was frightened. Quickly and intuitively she must have had an intimation of the price she would have to pay. God was calling on her to share with him a very intimate and solemn responsibility, and she knew enough about the flame of God's love to know that you cannot draw close to him or share his life with him without that flame searing your own heart. She knew enough of the ways of God to realize that responding to his call would mean a definite pattern as far as the future was concerned. The pattern would include pain, suffering, sacrifice, misunderstanding, criticism, the imputing of wrong motives. It is no wonder that she was frightened!

Another contributing factor to her hesitation and fear was a sense of personal inadequacy. She was not unaware of the nature of the responsibility she would be assuming —how her judgment and values and influence would play such an important part in the life of her Son. Who was she to take on a task of that magnitude? Any person worth his salt is filled with a sense of inadequacy when God calls him to do anything—God who is perfect and absolute and beautiful and true. To be a servant of God in any undertaking should fill one with fear and trembling, and Mary was no exception. On top of all this there was something else that was troubling her, and this was a very human reaction indeed. She had doubts as to the feasibility of the whole thing. "Then said Mary unto the angel, 'How shall this be, seeing I know not a man?'" (*Lk. 1:34*) It is such a very poignant scene, isn't it? This young girl caught up in a situation that has cosmic proportions and significance, and she reminds one of a lovely butterfly fluttering and frightened inside something too big for her to understand or to escape from.

And then we see the angel reassuring her, reminding her that this will be God's doing, that God has his own special ways, and that with God nothing shall be impossible. One has to smile at the argument the angel uses to prove this point. "Behold, thy cousin Elizabeth, she hath also conceived a son in her old age, and this is the sixth month with her, who was called barren." This picture of the archangel Gabriel almost pleading a case before the young girl, but doing so to reassure her and sustain her is one of the tenderest scenes I know.

I feel sure that not all of Mary's doubts and fears were cleared away. Indeed, I suspect that she carried some of them to her grave. But at least enough were cleared away to free her of their crippling and inhibiting power, and to release her for decision and action. "And Mary said,

'Behold the handmaid of the Lord; be it unto me according to thy word.' " *(Lk. 1:38)* So that in her response we see Mary moving from the area of hesitation and fear to the point of acceptance.

As we meditate on the nature of Mary's acceptance, we see what a difference this acceptance made in the future course of her life. For one thing, it meant a difference in priorities as far as her life was concerned. Before the angel's visit, Mary was engaged to be married. Her future would adhere to a familiar pattern. She would be a Jewish housewife, and her life would be her home and her family. The angel, however, ushered her into a new dimension. From the moment that she said, "Behold the handmaid of the Lord; be it unto me according to thy word," she was placing herself under a greater loyalty even than that of her family. Once a person arrives at the point of saying to God, "Be it unto me according to thy word," then all other loyalties become either secondary or supplemental. For when the primary law of your being is that God's will be done in you and through you, this is apt to lead you into painful byways where you will encounter strange and unfamiliar things. The person who lives by the prayer "Be it unto me according to thy word" is destined to arrive at a place called Gethsemane and from there move on to Calvary's hill. "There stood by the cross of Jesus, his mother." *(John 19:25)*

It takes courage to come to the place of acceptance. I believe that it takes greater courage than it does faith. "Now we see through a glass darkly." So that most of us find it easier to remain in the cowardly shadows of hesitation, doubt, and fear than to move on into the sharp glare of acceptance and commitment. "Behold the handmaid of the Lord; be it unto me according to thy word."

95

Open our eyes, O God, to see that thou dost not call a person to any task which, with thy help, is impossible of fulfillment. May we one day learn that thou really dost know what thou art doing. Then may we accept our own particular task in the spirit that we see Mary accepting hers; through Jesus Christ our Lord. Amen.

SAINT MARK THE EVANGELIST

April 25

Many of the disciples were older men—men of maturity and experience. And it was important during those years when the Christian faith and the Christian Church were being established that there should be this maturity and experience to call upon. But in the case of St. Mark there is the possibility that we are dealing with a more youthful man. In this meditation, then, let us consider the discipleship of the young.

Throughout the Church's history some of the greatest contributions to its life and work have been made by young men and young women. What are some of those qualities which are characteristic of the young and which help to make them valiant and ardent disciples?

One of the reasons, I think, why the young are especially sensitive and responsive to our Lord is that our Lord himself was a young man, and they are able to find in him a kindred spirit. Why? The first few lines of a poem by Percy gives us part of the answer:

> Delicious hurt is in the throb
> Of every ruby in youth's blood:
> Moonlight or love can call a sob,
> Or red trees in a drizzling wood.[9]

The young are responsive to our Lord because they are responsive to life—to all the wonder and beauty of life.

And who could know, better than our Lord, how wonderful and beautiful life is? So we see the young attracted to him because they realize that he feels deeply and intensely about things, as they do. Could the author of Ecclesiastes have had this in mind when he wrote:

> Remember now thy Creator
>   in the days of thy youth,
> While the evil days come not,
>   nor the years draw nigh,
> When thou shalt say
>   I have no pleasure in them. (*Eccles. 12:1*)

The young feel deeply and intensely about things—that is why they make good disciples. They are willing to espouse a cause, they are glad to follow a Saviour. They can believe in something strongly enough not only to act on their belief, but also to find pleasure in their action.

Another reason why the young can be such effective disciples, why they can be, as St. Paul said of Mark, "profitable to me for the ministry," is that they are willing to take risks. The older we become, the more cautious we become, the more insistent on assurances and certainties. Perhaps this is why people who do not marry when they are young seldom marry at all. Marriage requires real courage, a real act of faith, the willingness to take a chance. What would have happened to the Church and to the faith in those early years if men like Paul and Mark had not been willing to gamble, had refused to take such incredible risks because the outcome was so uncertain. Think of our missionary program today, both at home and abroad. Very little new work would ever be undertaken if some minister or congregation did not believe strongly enough in the cause to take some chances.

The young feel deeply and intensely, they are willing to act on faith, they are not afraid to give. One of the causes, it seems, of the frustration (with all its accompanying problems) of our youth today is that we do not permit them the opportunity of sacrifice. Even the Church has failed them in this matter, thinking more of what we could do for them than of what they might do for God. Surely much of the violence that we see erupting in our youth all over the world is because they see no answer to that deep need within themselves to sacrifice, to give themselves completely and lovingly to something worth while! They must give themselves to something, and when it is not to something good, then it will be to something evil. Have the Communists, perhaps, surpassed the Christians in this regard? Is that why their young are such potent disciples? Is it because they have been given a vision and a call to sacrifice?

To all young disciples our word must be: Long to give yourselves away, waste not your precious lives and blood in the service of that which hates and destroys. Betray not yourselves and your children in following after false gods. Lift your eyes to the Cross and to Christ and find in his service that which alone can bring peace and love.

Protect our youth, O God, in their response to life and to themselves. Help us to give them a vision that is great enough to satisfy their deep feeling, their faith, and their desire to give and to love. We ask this in the name of Christ our Lord. Amen.

SAINT PHILIP AND SAINT JAMES, APOSTLES

May 1

We are told in St. John's Gospel that when our Lord called Philip to be one of the twelve apostles, one of the first things Philip did was to try to share this wonderful thing that had happened to him with someone else. He sought out Nathanael "and said unto him, 'We have found him, of whom Moses in the law, and the prophets, did write, Jesus of Nazareth, the son of Joseph.' And Nathanael said unto him, 'Can there any good thing come out of Nazareth?' Philip saith unto him, 'Come and see.'" (*John 1:45-46*)

In this brief little scene we witness in miniature the whole pattern of the Christian missionary enterprise. We notice first of all that it begins where everything that is Christian should begin, namely with Christ. The record doesn't say that Philip found our Lord. It says just the opposite. It says that our Lord "went forth into Galilee and found Philip and said unto him, 'Follow me.'" (*John 1:43*) That great apostolic company, who were the first missionaries, did not discover our Lord. He discovered them and called them into a particular relationship with him. That was the way it began. But they found this relationship to be such a wonderful and exciting thing that they could not keep it to themselves, any more than you

100

can keep a ray of sunlight to yourself by trying to clutch it in your fist. This was something they simply had to share. So we see Philip running to tell Nathanael about it, just as Andrew had run to tell his brother Peter about it.

This, of course, is the very heart of Christian evangelism. We go out into all the world to tell people about Christ and to bring them into relationship with him, not primarily because he told us to do this, but chiefly because our relationship with him is too wonderful to keep to ourselves. This principle is true in all departments of life. You happen to look out the window and see a glorious sunset casting its flamboyant colors across the sky, and you call to whoever is in the house to run to share it with you. You turn on the radio and the Metropolitan Opera is singing *La Forza del Destino,* and you run to the phone to call someone you know would enjoy it. Our Lord called Philip to be his close companion, and this was something Philip could not keep to himself. He sought out Nathanael, wanting him to enjoy this relationship also. Nathanael, however, was not quite ready. His response was so typical of many of us when we are invited to share a really close relationship with our Lord. His response was one of hesitation, one of question, even to the extent of jesting about the announcement—"Can there any good thing come out of Nazareth?" Do we not hear ourselves uttering those same words when we are told something that seems too good to be true? Fearing that we might be disappointed we hesitate, we question, we stall for time. "Can there any good thing come out of Nazareth?" There is only one answer to a question like that. There is only one answer whenever our Lord is concerned. "Come and see."

We can seek out the Nathanaels of the world as did the Apostle Philip. We can speak to them as eloquently and as persuasively as possible about the joys of a loving relationship with Christ. We can try to overcome their defenses

101

of doubt and hesitation with every argument at our command. But sooner or later we reach the point where there is nothing for us to do but simply stretch forth our hand and say with Philip, "Come and see."

In giving this invitation, Philip was echoing the cry of the Psalmist uttered hundreds of years before: "O taste, and see, how gracious the Lord is." (*Ps. 34:8*) There is something universal in this cry which is true of all religious experience, but especially true of the Christian religion. Before we know how gracious our Lord is we must first taste and see. The joys and the mysteries of our faith are revealed only to those who are willing to put their hands to the Christian plow. "If any man will come after me let him deny himself, and take up his cross, and follow me." (*Matt. 16:24*) In other words, we can know Christ and we can love him only to the extent of our commitment to him. "Taste and see how gracious the Lord is."

We should not be at all surprised that this principle is true of the religious life because it is equally true in all departments of life. A musician can know and love great music only after he has first committed himself to the world of music; and his knowledge and his love grow in direct proportion to the growth of his commitment. A husband and wife can know the mysteries and the joys of the Sacrament of Marriage, the heights and the depths of home and family life, only after they have first committed themselves to that sacrament. "I, John, take thee, Mary, to my wedded wife, to have and to hold from this day forward, for better for worse, for richer for poorer, in sickness and in health, to love and to cherish, till death us do part." That is real commitment, and every married couple knows that the love and the cherishing grow only to the extent that this commitment is deepened and strengthened through the years.

We reach out to the Nathanaels of the world to tell them of the beauty and the love of Christ. Their response is often one of hesitation and doubt. "Can there any good thing come out of Nazareth?" Our answer to this question is an apostolic one. "Come and see."

O God, may we, who approach the flame of thy love like timid children fearful of being burned, learn that we can never really know thee or love thee until we are willing to take in our hands the Cross of thy dear Son and lift it up that men might come and see. Amen.

SAINT BARNABAS THE APOSTLE

June 11

Meditations usually deal with matters pertaining to the spiritual life. In our meditation today, however, we shall be considering the importance of things physical. God is the God of earth as well as of heaven. He is the God of our bodies as well as our souls, and it seems fitting on this day, when we salute the apostle who was so actively engaged in ministering to the physical needs of men, that we concern ourselves with the importance of physical things.

First, let us note, the importance physical rest may have for spiritual well-being. We forget sometimes how deeply related the life of the body is to the life of the mind and spirit. Modern psychiatry has done much to point out the relation between the mind and the body. Many ills are diagnosed as being psychosomatic. A disturbed mind or spirit can result in a sick body. The reverse is also true. A tired or overwrought body can result in a frayed mind and spirit. The noise, speed, and pressures of modern living all take their toll on our physical reserves. Many of us would say Amen to the lines in Percy's poem:

> I have a need of silence and of stars;
> Too much is said too loudly; I am dazed.
> The silken sound of whirled infinity
> Is lost in voices shouting to be heard.[10]

The importance of things like silence and stars; the importance of physical rest!

Second, let us consider the importance of physical security. This is brought home to us very vividly every time we experience an earthquake. It seems as though God has suddenly removed his hand from sustaining the universe. We are so accustomed to the earth being steady and secure under our feet, we take it so for granted that every now and then God has to shake us up a bit to remind us how helpless we would be without him.

This is also true of economic security. Only those who have been really poor and really in want can know how demoralizing great poverty can be. It can be disastrous as far as the spiritual life is concerned. Our Lord was aware of this when he included in his wonderful prayer the petition "Give us this day our daily bread." And again, when he said to the devil, "Man does not live by bread alone," he was not minimizing the importance of the bread. Man must live by something more than bread, yes, but he will not live long without bread. It has been suggested that there are no longer any poor people or rich people in this country, that everyone is sort of in-between. And yet we still seem to confront problems almost every day because of the anxiety that comes from economic insecurity.

If one feels that he has a vocation to the kind of renunciation practiced by our Lord, that is one thing. He can renounce family, friends, and home—the whole pattern of security that makes up the social fabric. But not many of us are called to that vocation. God did not intend for all of us to feel such a vocation. He needs families and homes and the vocation of the fireside and the hearth. This does not mean that in the midst of economic security we should not strive to keep the flame of renunciation alive in our hearts and in our lives, but this we can do while we are still fighting to see that all God's children are spared physical suffering and want.

The final thing I wish to point out is the importance of physical companionship. A few people now and then may achieve such a degree of sanctity or sin that they do not feel the need of human companionship. But most of us are made differently and we feel the need of the warm sun, the soft rain, the gentle wind, and the touch of a human hand. The poet expresses a universal longing when he turns to God and says,

> I sometimes think thou art my secret love;
>> But not tonight. . . . Tonight I have the need
> Of human tenderness; not hovering wings,
>> But one warm breast where I may lay my head
> And close my eyes.[11]

Here we touch one of the very cornerstones of the Christian faith. Listen to the way the apostles put it: "We are members one of another." (*Eph. 4:25*) "Bear ye one another's burdens." (*Gal. 6:2*) "If a man say I love God and hateth his brother he is a liar." (*I John 4:20*) Who is my neighbor? "A certain man went down from Jerusalem to Jericho and fell among thieves." (*Lk. 10:28-30*)

Over and over again, like the waves of the sea beating upon the shore this essential Christian theme is sounded. And unless those of us who make up the Christian family reach out unceasingly with the arms of our love to embrace, not just with our prayers, but with our human affection, those who need the support of a flesh and blood hand—unless we do this then everything else is so much "sound and fury, signifying nothing."

O God, may we, who hold a sacramental faith, know the importance of the outward and visible, and its relation to the inward and spiritual. May we reach out to the hungry and lonely people of the earth with physical food as well as spiritual, knowing that a healthy body helps create a healthy soul. We ask this in the name of him who ministered both to bodies and souls, Jesus Christ our Lord. Amen.

SAINT JOHN BAPTIST

June 24

There are certain points of similarity between the birth of St. John the Baptist and the birth of our Lord. In both cases we see the hand of God intervening into the lives of men. We see evidences of the supernatural breaking through into the realm of the natural. Surrounding the birth of both of them is an aura of mystery and miracle. Our Lord's mother was a young virgin. St. John's mother was an old lady. For, as the angel reminds us, "With God nothing shall be impossible." (*Lk. 1:37*) Mary was so moved at the thought of the child she would bear that she sang a lovely song, "My soul doth magnify the Lord, and my spirit hath rejoiced in God my Saviour." (*Lk. 1:46-47*) John's father, Zacharias was equally moved at the birth of his son, and he, too, left us a lovely song, "Blessed be the Lord God of Israel; for he hath visited and redeemed his people . . . And thou, child, shalt be called the prophet of the Highest: for thou shalt go before the face of the Lord to prepare his ways." (*Lk. 1:68,76*)

God exercised extreme care, not only in the matter of the Incarnation, but also in the choice of him who would prepare the minds and hearts of men for the Incarnation. One reason for this is quite obvious. Anything as important as the coming of God into the world for the purpose of saving the world deserves great care in the matter of preparation. (And this, of course, is the theme of the Advent Season.) But there is another reason why God chose John the Baptist. In doing so, he was taking pains to see that the Christian drama of Redemption should be identified with, and in the mainstream of, the great prophetic tradition of the Old Testament. John the Baptist was truly a great prophet, in the noble tradition of Moses and Elijah, and to choose such a man as the forerunner and herald of the Christian faith and the Christian Church was God's way of saying that there is a real place and a real need in that faith and in that Church for prophets. And when we look about us at the world today we would do well to pray that God would raise up in our time some great prophet whose voice would ring as clear and as true as did the voice of John the Baptist calling upon the people of Israel to repent and turn to God.

But before we can pray effectively for such a prophet, we need to know what we are praying for, what a prophet is supposed to be and to do. I would say that the chief function of the prophet is first, to discern the character and the will of God, and then to proclaim that character and will, relating it to every situation in life. This means that the prophet must be also a good listener. Before he can say with any conviction, "Thus saith the Lord," he must first be able to hear what the Lord says. And to do this he must listen. God speaks to different prophets in different ways. Some of them, like John the Baptist and Elijah, have to withdraw to the desert and the mountain to hear God speak in a still small voice. Some of them, like the princely Isaiah, listen better in the atmosphere of the Temple. "In the year that King Uzziah died I saw also the Lord sitting upon a throne, high and lifted up, and his train filled the Temple." (*Is. 6:1*) Some of them, like one Episcopal priest in New York, hear God's voice in a dirty, crowded slum apartment where the landlord of these Puerto Rican tenants has turned off the light and heat. The important thing is not how or where the voice of God is heard, but that those called to the prophetic ministry listen to his voice.

Having listened, the prophet must then proclaim what he hears, and this, of course, requires great courage. It wasn't easy or pleasant for John the Baptist to accuse King Herod of living in sin for taking his brother's wife. But John knew that God is a God of moral law; therefore, that any violation of that law is an offense in God's eyes. John discerned that aspect of the character and will of God and was fearless in proclaiming it. Think of the great prophet Amos, who was so shocked at the social and economic injustices in Israel, knowing that these things are an offense both to the justice and mercy of God, that he pronounced the doom of Israel, even saying that God would use the enemies of Israel, the Assyrians, to bring her to her knees. (*Amos 2—3*)

One thing that all the great prophets have discovered, both Christian and Jewish, is that God cares about the welfare of all his children. This is the spiritual structure of the universe. So that any form of social, economic, and racial injustice is bound to end in disaster. And I wonder if the events on the international scene cannot be interpreted as the judgment and, perhaps, the impatience of God. The Flood, at the time of Noah, suggests that there is such a thing as a limit to God's patience, and perhaps as he looks at the plight of many of his children today in India, Africa, and the southern United States of America, we can hear him saying, "How much longer do you think I am willing to stand for all this? Repent ye while there is time!"

Raise up in our time, we beseech thee, of God, some great prophet who, having listened to thy voice and discerned thy holy will, will proclaim it fearlessly to all men. Strengthen our resistance to all forms of injustice and assist us as we strive to achieve brotherhood among men; through Jesus Christ our Lord. Amen.

SAINT PETER THE APOSTLE

June 29

One of the most fascinating characters in all history is the fisherman Simon Peter. And one of the greatest contrasts that could be found in the study of a personality is seen in the difference between the Peter we find in the Gospels, and the Peter we meet in the Acts of the Apostles. It is hard to believe they are the same man. In the Gospels he appears before us in not a very favorable light. He is vacillating, impulsive, unstable. At one moment he cries out to our Lord, "Thou art the Christ, the son of the living God." The next moment he denies even knowing him. But when we turn to the Acts of the Apostles, the Peter that we encounter there is as steady as a rock. He is a man of conviction, authority, and eloquence. It is evident, therefore, that Peter was not always a great man. He is a study in the transformation of weakness into greatness. And in this meditation we shall try to see wherein the sources of his greatness lie.

One of the chief sources, I would say, is the fact that Peter was capable of contrition. And here we see the great difference between Peter and Judas Iscariot. Both men betrayed our Lord. There is no mistake about that. Judas, however, could not accept himself and his guilt so he killed himself. Peter, on the other hand, saw himself and his guilt for the first time when, after the terrible denial, our Lord turned and looked upon Peter. And when Peter's eyes met our Lord's, it was like having a searchlight turned into the depth of his soul. He saw himself with all his blustering self-assurance, his impulsive advances, and his hasty retreats; and when the awareness of what he had done bore down upon him, we are told that he went out and wept bitterly. Between Judas and Peter we see the difference between remorse and contrition. Remorse is always self-centered—it is ego-centered; it says in effect, "How could *I* have done a thing like that?" One is really more sorry about oneself, more remorseful about the revelation of oneself caused by the offense, than grieved about the offense itself. Contrition, on the other hand, is God-centered. One says, in effect, "What a terrible thing so to wound the heart of God!" Contrition is the desire to make amends, to offer some atonement, some reparation. Judas's suicide was not an act of atonement; it was an act of despair, despair about himself. If he had not been quite so ego-centric, if his mind and heart had been more God-centered than self-centered, then, like Peter, he would have tried somehow to make it up to God.

There was no humility and no generosity in Judas, at least not with himself. At the outset there was not much humility in Peter, but there was generosity, and because of that he was able to be generous with himself, he was able to accept himself. Humility was a slow and painful lesson for Peter to learn, but he learned it step by step. For everytime he was so loudly and excessively sure of himself our Lord would bring him to his knees. Remember the time when seeing our Lord, he started out so confidently to walk on the water? Only a step or two, and down he went. He had shifted his attention from our Lord to himself, and concern about himself. Again, when our Lord talked with his disciples after the Last Supper, speaking of his betrayal and death, and said that all his disciples would forsake him, Peter cried out, "Lord I am

113

ready to go with thee, both into prison and to death."
Poor Peter! The words were hardly out of his mouth
when the cock began to crow! But as he grew in humility,
he grew in the grace of contrition; and this is one of the
clues to his greatness.

A man who is capable of contrition is also capable of
changing, and herein lies the second clue to Peter's greatness. As we said a moment ago, contrition bears in its
hands the desire and the intent to lead a new and better
life. And when the desire is strong and real, the change
is bound to occur. One of the reasons why Peter became
the great man that we see in the Acts of the Apostles is
because he wanted to become that man. And while it is
true that in the Gospels we see Peter following our Lord
afar off, at least his face is turned in the direction of
greatness.

The real change in Peter's life, however, was brought
about not by his own desire and efforts. The real change
was accomplished by God. Indeed, are not all the real
changes in our lives wrought by God? We may, like Peter,
do everything in our power to pave the way and set the
stage. We can join the disciples in prayer and supplica-
tion, meeting "with one accord in one place." But when
the real transformation takes place it will come through
the "rushing mighty wind" and "the tongues of fire" of
God. Peter was capable of changing and becoming a different man because he surrendered himself to the transforming power of God!

But the most important clue as far as Peter is concerned
is the fact that he was capable of great love. Let us return
for a moment to the scene we mentioned earlier—that
almost unbearable scene of Peter's denial when our Lord
turned and looked upon Peter. Kierkegaard asks,

> What was the nature of that glance? Was it one of in-
> dignation? Was it one of injured feelings? Or was it the
> beseeching, compassionate glance that a mother gives to a

child who is in danger? For indeed, Peter was the one who was really in danger; it is a terrible thing to betray a friend! Jesus did not see his cause lost if Peter did not hasten to help him, but he saw Peter lost if he (Jesus) did not hasten to save him. He did not say, Peter must first be changed and become another man before I can love him. He said just the opposite. He said, Peter is Peter, and I love him, as I see him now, at this moment, when he betrays and denies me.[12]

Peter was never able to forget our Lord's response of love at that moment of danger and crisis. To me, that was the real turning point of Peter's conversion, the chief factor that transformed him from weakness into greatness. For throughout the rest of his days we see Peter trying to return something of that quality of love which he witnessed in our Lord's eyes that dreadful night of betrayal. "We love him, because he first loved us." (*I John 4:19*)

O God, who hast prepared for those who love thee such good things as pass man's understanding; Pour into our hearts such love toward thee, that we, loving thee above all things, may obtain thy promises, which exceed all that we can desire; through Jesus Christ our Lord. Amen.

(Book of Common Prayer)

SAINT JAMES THE APOSTLE

July 25

Our knowledge of Saint James is limited but there are certain references which give us an idea of his place in the apostolic company. We know, for example, that together with his brother John, he assisted his father Zebedee in what was apparently a fairly prosperous fishing business. We know also that when he responded to the call to follow our Lord, he was admitted to the closest and most intimate circle, the group—James, Peter, and John —who were present at the Transfiguration and who were chosen to share the agony in Gethsemane. We know, finally, that James was killed by the sword in Herod's attempt to stamp out the new faith. These are the pictures that we encounter of James in the pages of Holy Scripture. This is the story of his discipleship. As we review the story, we might learn some lessons which are relevant to our own sense of discipleship.

The first picture that we have of James shows him in the context of his home, his family, and his business. It is a picture of security and affection. His physical and social needs are well provided for. He is a substantial and respected member of the community. Suddenly he is asked to turn his back on all this, to give up the security he has worked so hard to achieve and to sever the ties with those who are near and dear. So that the first lesson we learn from the story of his discipleship is something of the cost involved.

It will be argued that James was called to a particular vocation, a vocation for the very few, and that most of us have to try to fulfill our discipleship in and through our homes, our families, and our business. This may be true; but if there isn't in our discipleship some element of renunciation, some degree of sacrifice, some evidence of a real cost involved, then it can hardly be called Christian discipleship. "Whosoever will come after me, let him deny himself, and take up his cross, and follow me." (*Mk. 8:34*)

It is so tempting to become "at ease in Zion," and while we certainly need the vocation of the home and hearth, there is danger, I believe, when the Christian vocation becomes so domestic in its emphasis, that the first question committees often ask about a prospective new minister or priest is "Does he have a wife and family?"

Our second picture of St. James is as a member of the inner circle to which we referred at the beginning. What cost did that privilege involve? What does love always demand of those who draw close enough to take love by the hand? We mentioned that James was present at the Transfiguration *and* at Gethsemane. That is the way with love. One must share not only the glory but also the pain. Could this be the trouble with many of our marriages today and the cause of so much divorce? As long as it is "for better" all goes well, but when it is "for worse" the shallowness of the love is exposed.

Our Lord is so often portrayed as a person of sweetness and light, that one might easily lose sight of the darker moments—the moments of loneliness and discouragement which those who were closest to him would have to witness and not be able to dispel. It costs a great deal to draw close to truth, and endure its searching gaze. It isn't easy to look upon a thing so beautiful that it brings you to your knees. But to draw close to our Lord and the quality of his love, the cost is everything!

This is made clear in our final picture of James when he offered the ultimate that man can give—his life. What a contrast there is between this final scene when James staggers under Herod's sword, and the first scene among the fishing boats of Galilee! Gone is the home, the family, the security. No longer can be heard the laughter of children as they play along the shore. Instead of the song of a wandering bird, the sunlight on the water, there is now the clash of steel, the darkness of prison and of death.

We need to be reminded of this quality of discipleship, this degree of courage, and of love which is willing to draw close to our Lord and to walk with him the whole way! Percy sums it up very poignantly in these verses:

> I love to think of them at dawn
> Beneath the frail pink sky
> Casting their nets in Galilee
> And fish-hawks circling by.
>
> Casting their nets in Galilee
> Just off the hills of brown,
> Such happy, simple fisherfolk
> Before the Lord walked down.
>
> Contented, peaceful fishermen,
> Before they ever knew
> The peace of God that filled their hearts
> Brim-full and broke them too.
>
> Young John who trimmed the flapping sail,
> Homeless, in Patmos died.
> Peter who hauled the teeming net,
> Head-down, was crucified.
>
> The peace of God it is no peace,
> But strife closed in the sod.
> Yet, brothers, pray for but one thing
> The marvellous peace of God.[13]

Revive in our time, O God, the quality of discipleship which is willing to forsake all and follow thee. Deliver us from the snare of a domesticated Christ and a domesticated Church. Give us prophets and saints, martyrs, and men of zeal for thy kingdom; through Jesus Christ our Lord. Amen.

THE TRANSFIGURATION OF CHRIST

August 6

The Transfiguration is one of the most beautiful celebrations of the year. The very word "Transfiguration" is such a lovely one, and the idea which it suggests is so very appealing. With our frail bodies and tarnished souls, how wonderful it would be if we could suddenly be transfigured, as our Lord was, into radiant and shining creatures of such transparent beauty and purity that our brightness would surpass that of the sun!

We are told that our Lord went up into the mountain to pray, taking with him Peter and James and John, "And as he prayed, the fashion of his countenance was altered." (*Lk. 9:29*) Isn't that a beautiful line? And doesn't it suggest to us, whose faces are so often sad and anxious and harassed, how our countenances may be altered? "And as he prayed the fashion of his countenance was altered, and his raiment was white and glistering." There is no way of defining the moment of Transfiguration which our Lord experienced on the mountain, no way of analyzing it or explaining it. For the closer we draw to it the greater does the brightness become, so much so that we are blinded by its dazzling beauty. We seem to leave the world of the natural and to enter that mysterious realm of the supernatural, inhabited by the angels and archangels and the whole company of heaven. Apparently it is a moment of such complete consecration and consuming prayer that the veil between the physical and the spiritual, between the temporal and the eternal, is removed, and we see the blending of both worlds into one. That moment on the mountain teaches us what a transfiguring experience prayer can be. The Gospel tells us that so completely was our Lord caught up into that realm which transcends time and space that two of the ancient leaders of Israel, Moses, and Elias, appeared to stand on either side of him as he prayed—Moses representing the Law, Elias the Prophets, and our Lord the fulfillment of both.

May we turn now to Peter and observe for a few moments the nature of his response to that vision on the mountain. What a very human response it was! For one thing, Peter slept through a good part of the vision. You and I would probably have done the same. The hour was late and he was tired. But we are shocked to think that he would do such a thing. We feel the same way we do when we go to a great play and are watching a gifted performance and suddenly a man in front of us begins to snore. In a sense it is a sacrilege, but worse than that it is sad to think of how much the man is missing. Peter missed so many of the great moments in our Lord's life! But fortunately he didn't miss the entire experience on the Mount of Transfiguration. Suddenly he awoke and saw the Lord in all his glory. And "Peter said unto Jesus, 'Master it is good for us to be here.'" (Lk. 9:33) Can you imagine the feeling of awe and wonder that this simple fisherman must have felt as he gazed at our Lord's transcendent beauty? He probably felt the same way Joseph felt as he stood at the manger in Bethlehem. One poet has described Joseph, the carpenter, as he gazed at the infant Jesus, thus:

After the Wise Men went, and the strange star
Had faded out, Joseph the father sat

121

Watching the sleeping Mother and the Babe,
And thinking stern, sweet thoughts the long night through.

"Ah, what am I, that God has chosen me
To bear this blessed burden, to endure
Daily the Presence of this loveliness,
To guide this Glory that shall guide the world?

"Brawny these arms to win him bread, and broad
This bosom to sustain her. But my heart
Quivers in lonely pain before that Beauty
It loves—and serves—and cannot understand!" [14]

Peter, no doubt, felt the same way. "Master, it is good for us to be here."

But then Peter goes on to say something which again is typically human, and in a sense, somewhat spoils the beauty of the moment. He says, "Let us make three tabernacles; one for thee, and one for Moses, and one for Elias, not knowing what he said." (*Lk. 9:33*) Indeed, he didn't know what he said, for he was asking for the impossible. For one thing, he was seeking to prolong the moment of Transfiguration. "Master it is good for us to be here." Let us stay here where everything is so lovely and not return to the ugliness and sin of the world! Peter should have known—for he had lived long enough to learn this lesson—that moments of breath-taking beauty and intensity cannot be prolonged. Indeed, their very fleetingness and transiency is part of the essence of their beauty! Neither our Lord nor his disciples would have been able to endure, either physically or emotionally, the Transfiguration experience had it been extended and prolonged. It was one of those rare moments of vision that God does vouchsafe to us now and then, but it must go as quickly as it comes. Such moments of vision are not given us to pickle and preserve. When with Peter we say, "Let us build three tabernacles," we propose, in effect to somehow box this all up so that it can never get away from us. The Holy Land is filled with examples of this very thing. There is a place, certainly, for holy shrines, but so often they are spoiled through an absence of imagination.

Some things can be pickled and preserved, like food and money. Others cannot. And the Spirit that filled our Lord's life is one of the things that cannot be boxed up. Try to clutch it and keep it yourself, and it dies. The only way it can live is when it is let loose and given away. Our Lord's Spirit is like a bird that can sing the sweetest music as long as it is free to sing for the whole world. Put the bird in a cage and the music dies.

We thank thee, O God, for those moments of vision, those moments of Transfiguration, without which man would perish. May we draw from them all the inspiration and refreshment of Spirit which they are able to provide. Then may we quickly try to share them with others, for the only way we can keep them is to give them away. This we ask in the name of Jesus Christ, our Lord. Amen.

SAINT BARTHOLOMEW THE APOSTLE

August 24

Of the twelve apostles that our Lord chose to be his close companions there are some about whom we know a good deal. The record contains various scenes in which they appear; we are told something of their background, their character, and their work. But there are others about whom we know practically nothing. No mention is made of anything that they said or did. This happens to be the case with St. Bartholomew, whose feast we celebrate today. His name is listed in the first three Gospels as being one of the twelve apostles. Beyond that, we are told nothing.

But tradition has suggested that Bartholomew is the same person who, in St. John's Gospel, is referred to as Nathanael. And we do know something about him. Our Lord himself tells us what he was like. "Jesus saw Nathanael coming to him, and saith of him, 'Behold an Israelite indeed, in whom is no guile.'" (*John 1:47*) The dictionary says that a guileless person is an innocent person. So that if we wish to understand the nature and character of Nathanael Bartholomew, we must consider this matter of innocence.

We do not mean by innocence the state of being that existed in the Garden of Eden before Adam and Eve ate the forbidden fruit. They didn't know there was such a thing as evil until after they had taken that fatal bite.

124

This is perhaps why the fall of man has been referred to as the fall upwards. It ushered mankind into a new dimension of being, a dimension in which he knows the existence of good and evil and the difference between the two. By innocence, therefore, we do not mean ignorance of evil, but rather that purity of heart which, seeing the evil, despises and rejects it. In other words, we think of innocence as that degree of sanctity which brings one to the point of loving that which is good and hating that which is evil.

We must make a distinction between the innocent person and the naïve person. A naïve person is sometimes simply too stupid to be aware of a threatening evil. It isn't a matter of sanctity but simple-mindedness. This is not what we mean by innocence.

We have to admit, however, that some people are born with purer hearts than others, and in a few rare cases, the purity never deserts them. They seem to be constitutionally unable to think or say or do a malicious thing. St. John, the beloved Disciple, seems to have been such a person. Nathanael, perhaps, was another. "Behold an Israelite, indeed, in whom is no guile."

But most of us are not as innocent as we wish we were; we are not as pure in heart as we would like to be. Is there anything we can do about it? There seem to be schools for everything else; what about a school that would specialize in purity of heart? Not where we would try to recapture the lost innocence of childhood—an innocence that is often greatly exaggerated and romanticized—but where we could cultivate the mature innocence of sanctity. Such a school would offer at least two main courses. One of these would be a course in concentration.

Purity of heart, Kierkegaard reminds us, is "to will one thing." It is to streamline one's affections and desires so completely in the direction of God that our fractured and vacillating souls become integrated in him. Integration is a prelude to integrity, and integrity is another name for purity. Most of us are torn between so many conflicting desires! We want to eat our cake and still have it. We would like to move, however, from the distractions and tensions of the many into the more serene realm of oneness, the realm of purity. We long, with Thomas Wolfe, "to see a forest in a leaf, the whole earth in a single face." We could do with a course in concentration!

A second course that the school would be sure to offer would be a course in association. We all know what it means when we speak of guilt by association. But there is also such a thing as innocence by association. If the bad habits and evil natures of our associates can have a contaminating influence, so can good habits and purity of heart have a healing influence. We would do well to expose ourselves more than we do to this type of influence. Not just with the company that we keep but in all avenues of life—the things that we read, the pictures that we see, the music that we hear. As St. Paul urges in his letter to the Philippians, "Whatsoever things are true, whatsoever things are honest, whatsoever things are just, whatsoever things are pure, whatsoever things are lovely, whatsoever things are of good report . . . think on these things." (*Phil. 4:8*)

We *can* do something about the purity of our hearts! I have suggested only two ways—the ways of concentration and association. There are others that may appeal to you more. None of them are easy ways, but the reward is out of all proportion to our feeble effort. Our Lord tells us what the reward will be: "Blessed are the pure in heart: for they shall see God." (*Matt. 5:8*)

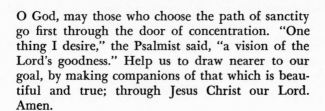

O God, may those who choose the path of sanctity go first through the door of concentration. "One thing I desire," the Psalmist said, "a vision of the Lord's goodness." Help us to draw nearer to our goal, by making companions of that which is beautiful and true; through Jesus Christ our Lord. Amen.

SAINT MATTHEW, APOSTLE AND EVANGELIST

September 21

In our consideration of St. James and others of the apostles, we noted the cost of discipleship—the sacrifices they were called upon to make, the loss of material comfort and security; the separation from home, family, and friends; the offering of their very lives. This is part of the price the disciple is called upon to pay.

In our discussion of St. Matthew we shall consider some of the rewards of discipleship. We shall see that it isn't all sacrifice, suffering, and pain, but that there are also very real and great compensations. This does not mean that Matthew was spared any of the cost. We see him paying in full just as all the others were called upon to do. But this should not blind us to the beauty of the rewards. We shall mention only three.

For one thing, Matthew found the companionship which is reserved for those who care. His life—before our Lord turned it upside down—was obviously comfortable and secure, but it must have been, I feel, a lonely life. As a publican and tax-collector, he was a social and religious outcast in the eyes of his people the Jews. I doubt if the social stigma concerned him a great deal, but being, at least potentially, a deeply religious person he would feel very keenly the absence of spiritual companionship.

Suddenly, into the midst of this isolation and loneliness, a voice says, "Follow me," and we see Matthew joining the ranks of a little company composed of people who care.

Of course, the deepest spiritual bond that unites these men as brothers is the personality of him whom they believe to be, in a very special way, the anointed one of God. Thus it is because they care first and foremost about God, about the nature of his character and will, that we find the true source of their fellowship. Caring about God leads them to care about one another in that gentle, solicitous way which they see reflected in the Master. Gradually, they move out from this center until they come to care for all men, knowing that all men are God's children and their brothers. This companionship, therefore, is one of the rewards of discipleship—companionship with those who care.

Secondly, Matthew was given the insight which is open to those who serve. In the account of the marriage feast at Cana we are told that when the water which our Lord had turned into wine was brought to the ruler of the feast, he "knew not whence it was: (but the servants which drew the water knew)." (*John 2:9*) So often those who serve behind the scenes are vouchsafed insights which are denied those whom they serve. Could it not be that some of the very perceptive and wonderful insights which our Lord revealed were made known to him in and through his capacity as minister and servant? In that very tender scene following the Last Supper, when our Lord washed the disciples' feet, we think usually of the effect of that act upon the disciples. What about the effect which it had on our Lord? What new insights and avenues of grace were opened to him as he knelt in such complete humility? Similar rewards of insight and grace must have come to Matthew as he assumed his role of servant, the role which is of the very essence of discipleship.

Finally, Matthew enjoyed the fulfillment which is offered to those who give. In his poem "Self-Protection," D. H. Lawrence speaks of the nightingale's "giving himself away" in song which is the "culminating point of his existence."

What is true of the nightingale is equally true of man, and especially true in his role as Christian disciple. The culminating point of the disciple's existence is in his giving himself away, and while the cost may be great, involving sacrifice, suffering, and death, we must remember that "the disciple is not above his master"; and as we gaze at our Lord with arms outstretched and hear him say, "It is finished," we must try to grasp some idea of the sense of fulfillment which he knew at that moment and which must have made the terrible cost seem worth-while.

Almighty God, our heavenly Father, vouchsafe to us a vision not only of the cost of discipleship but also of its rewards. May the lonely people of the earth find companionship in the company of those who care. May they gain the insights reserved for those who serve. May they enjoy the fulfillment which is offered to those who give. With these rewards before us, may we approach our discipleship with greater zeal, courage, and hope; through Jesus Christ our Lord. Amen.

SAINT MICHAEL AND ALL ANGELS

September 29

One of my favorite stories in the Old Testament is the story of the prophet, Elisha, who had been very successful in warning his people the Israelites about the attacks of the Syrian hosts. The King of Syria was determined to capture the prophet, and therefore sent a great army to lay siege to the city of Dothan, where the prophet was staying. When the servant of Elisha arose one morning and saw that the city was surrounded with the horses and chariots of the enemy, he rushed to his master and cried, "What shall we do?" Elisha answered his servant and said, "Fear not, for they that be with us are more than they that be with them. And Elisha prayed and said, Lord, I pray thee, open his eyes that he may see. And the Lord opened the eyes of the young man and he saw, and behold, the mountain was full of horses and chariots of fire 'round about Elisha!" (*II Kings 6:16-17*) The Lord vouchsafed to the young man a glimpse of that great company of the heavenly host which is always about each of us to strengthen and sustain us, but which we are too blind to see.

Today is the Feast of St. Michael and All Angels, and we shall try, for a moment at least, to brush away some of the scales that form so quickly upon our spiritual eyes, that we may stand at attention as the Angels and Archangels

131

go marching by "in solemn troops and sweet societies."

The observance of this festival tells us, first of all, something about God. It reminds us that he is a King, that he is a Being of infinite majesty. This is something we are apt to lose sight of in this age of the so-called common man. It is not easy for us to say to a person, "Your Majesty." We feel awkward when we try to observe the ceremonial customary in the presence of a reigning monarch. The lovely curtsy that our young girls used to perform with such grace is almost a thing of the past. Now, instead of referring to God as King of Kings and Lord of Lords, we speak of him as "the guy upstairs!" What a contrast between this cheap and flippant approach and that in John Milton's majestic poem "On the Morning of Christ's Nativity":

> But see! the Virgin blest
> Hath laid her Babe to rest;
>   Time is our tedious song should here have ending:
> Heaven's youngest-teemed Star
> Hath fixed her polished car,
>   Her sleeping Lord with handmaid lamp attending;
> And all about the courtly stable
> Bright-harnessed Angels sit in order serviceable.

We need to be reminded of the Majesty of God—of the fact that he is a King!

The observance of this festival also tells us something about heaven. It speaks to us of the infinite variety that is found in God's heavenly kingdom. One of the things that fascinates me so about life in the world is the rich variety that we encounter here. The incredible things that are found at the bottom of the sea, the artistry of a snowflake, the color of a butterfly, the distinctive difference that exists in every human soul! If this is true of the natural sphere, it is much more true of the supernatural sphere. And when we speak of the Angels and Archangels, we are referring to the variety of heaven. This thought, it seems to me, is good for our humility, for man is always inclined to put himself in the center of the picture, even when he thinks of heaven. There are people who think that heaven is a special place which God has designed for the future happiness of the human race. It is good for us to realize that man is not the most important inhabitant of heaven. There are also the Angels and Archangels, the Cherubim and Seraphim, and countless other orders of beings who may be much closer to the Throne of God than we will!

There's something else this holy day tells us about heaven. It means we're going to have to brush up on our manners a bit, for God is a King and heaven is a majestic kingdom. In God's presence we are told the Cherubim and Seraphim cover their faces when they cry, Holy, Holy, Holy. The Angels and Archangels fold their bright wings as they prostrate themselves before the throne of God. This is going to mean quite an adjustment for those of us who are unwilling to perform even the simplest courtesies in the exercise of our worship.

Finally and briefly, the observance of this feast tells us something about life in the world. It tells us that there is much less difference, much less separation between heaven and earth than we realize. Heaven is not a place —it is a quality of being. It is a matter of values. It is an atmosphere of adoration and love. And the important thing to remember about the angels is that they are not restricted to the supernatural realm. The place where you are sitting is filled with their bright presence, could you but see. The air about you is singing with the rush of their wings, could you but hear.

Therefore with Angels and Archangels, and with all the company of heaven, we laud and magnify thy glorious Name, evermore praising thee, and saying,

Holy, Holy, Holy, Lord God of Hosts;
heaven and earth are full of thy glory.
Glory be to thee, O Lord Most High. Amen.

SAINT LUKE THE EVANGELIST

October 18

In this twofold vocation of doctor and missionary we learn the secret of the Christian life and faith. Somewhere along the line, in the history of our religion, a great divorce took place. It was the divorce between the material things of life and the spiritual things. I shall not attempt to probe into the background of this divorce or to examine all the causes which brought it about. Suffice it to say that the divorce did take place and the break was so strong and deep that people began to think in terms of two separate worlds of reality—one of them concerned with physical things, things like our bodies, our food, and our money. The other had to do with spiritual things— things like our prayers, our worship, and our souls.

I can think of no greater tragedy in the history of mankind than this divorce, for the results are evident all around us. God has been separated from his material creation. Religion has become a Sunday affair, something that has to do with special clothes, with hymns and sermons and prayers that we say for an hour or so in church. The body has been separated from the soul, and as a result both body and soul are restless and starved, and they walk through dry places seeking rest. This they can never find until the divorce has been healed, and there is a reunion —a remarriage of body and soul.

It is strange that this could ever have happened in the Christian religion, for the central fact of our faith is the Incarnation—that great pronouncement of the marriage vows between the spiritual and physical. The whole point of our Lord's life is that the divine and the human are met and married in his Person. And as we watch our Lord in the days of his ministry we never see him departmentalizing that ministry into either physical or spiritual needs. He came to make men whole, and to be whole involves the body and the soul. He knew that many of man's physical ailments are the result of spiritual disorders, and vice versa, so that often in his healing we hear him say, "Thy sins be forgiven thee," or "Thy faith hath made thee whole."

St. Luke was a doctor and a physician, and therefore he was concerned with the diseases of mankind. But he was also an evangelist, a missionary, so that when he tried to heal someone he ministered to the man's whole being—not just his body, but also his soul. The two are so closely related as far as health is concerned. When you walk about the streets of any town in this country, you see many offices with neat little signs that say, John Jones, M.D. Wouldn't it be wonderful if now and then you came upon a sign that said, John Jones, Physician and Evangelist! But instead, you go to see your doctor for your physical ailments. Then you cross the street and go to a minister or to a psychiatrist for your spiritual ailments. More of our doctors should also be evangelists, and more of our clergymen should also be physicians and psychiatrists. This might help somewhat to heal the great divorce, and bridge the gulf between the body and the soul.

Religion is concerned with the totality of life. It has as much to say about the material world as it does about the spiritual world, because both worlds are God's and therefore they are really one. Our Lord was always concerned with and spoke to every area of a man's life—the

material as well as the spiritual—for he was concerned
with the whole man. He came to make them whole. And
may I say, there can never be wholeness in a person's life
where God does not come first! It is just as simple as that.
I'll leave it to your own conscience to decide where he
stands on your list of priorities.

Almighty God, who didst inspire thy servant Saint
Luke, the Physician, to set forth in the Gospel the
love and healing power of thy Son; Manifest in thy
Church the like power and love, to the healing of
our bodies and our souls; through the same thy
Son Jesus Christ our Lord. Amen.

(Book of Common Prayer)

SAINT SIMON AND SAINT JUDE, APOSTLES

October 28

In meditating on the saints, the Christian usually attempts to paint something in the way of an individual portrait of the saint. Since the record is rather sparse as far as St. Simon and St. Jude are concerned, in this meditation let us consider rather the concept of sainthood in the general sense.

If someone were to ask us to define a saint, I am sure that we would come up with many different and interesting answers. Some would think at once of the great giants of the Faith—men like Peter, John, Paul, Francis of Assisi; women like Mary Magdalene, Teresa, Catherine. The New Testament, however, uses the word "saint" in a different category. When Paul says in his letters, "All the saints salute you," he is referring to all members of the Church who are trying to be faithful to their Lord, Jesus Christ.

We would do well to try to recapture this concept of sainthood. As Paul reminds us, all Christians are called to be saints. This is our essential vocation, and just because the Church has given official recognition and status only to the outstanding saints of the ages, does not mean that you and I are relieved of our responsibility in this matter. Therefore, may I suggest this simple definition, which I believe might help us as we try to fulfill our role of sainthood. The definition is inspired by a line in St. Paul's second letter to Timothy. You may remember it. St. Paul, in prison in Rome, knows that he has but a short time to live, and thinking of his life and his ministry, he sums it up in these words: "I have fought a good fight. I have finished my course. I have kept the faith." (*II Tim. 4:7*) The definition is this: A saint is a Christian soldier. And we shall use this definition as the theme for this meditation, with special emphasis on the Christian soldier as a fighter.

Unfortunately, he does not often appear so, for in spite of some of the more militant hymns that we sing like "Onward Christian Soldiers, Marching as to War," I'm afraid that not many congregations would strike much terror in the heart of anyone, to say nothing of causing the devil himself to tremble! And yet, every Christian Baptism is a declaration of war, when we promise to fight against the world, the flesh, and the devil, and to continue Christ's faithful soldier until our life's end! When St. Paul said, "I have fought a good fight," he was not just making a pretty speech. His words were quite literal and in dead earnest. And since the world and human nature are not a great deal different now than they were in his time, we might do well to consider some of the aspects of his fight and see what bearing they have on our vocation as Christian soldiers.

In the first place, St. Paul did not make the mistake that soldiers sometimes make of underestimating the power of the enemy. Evil was an objective and demonic reality for St. Paul—a thing so ruthless and so subtle that without God's help man wouldn't stand a chance in his struggle against it. "We wrestle not against flesh and blood, but against principalities, against powers, against the rulers of the darkness of this world, against spiritual wickedness in high places." (*Eph. 6:12*) And for St. Paul, there was

139

no area of life that was safe from the invasion of this enemy. We see Paul waging his battle on three major fronts.

The first battlefield was that of his own soul, for after our Lord called him to be an apostle we see him spending several years in his own spiritual warfare before he would undertake so solemn a task—years of testing and examining his motives, years of purifying, strengthening, dedicating. The battlefield that lies within a man's soul is one from which he can never withdraw or retreat, for that is the devil's favorite meeting ground. St. Paul, who knew so profoundly and so intimately the power of the enemy in this area cried out, "The good that I would, I do not; but the evil which I would not, that I do." (*Rom. 7:19*) Our Lord himself spent much of his time on the same battlefield. The temptations in the wilderness at the beginning of his ministry and the agony in the garden at the end, testify to the persistence of the devil on this particular front.

The second great battlefield that St. Paul knew was within the Church itself. His letters are filled with his struggles against those who were trying to make the Church something other than our Lord intended it to be. One of his greatest and most significant fights was with the apostles themselves. Some of them wanted to insist that before a man could become a Christian, he must first submit to the Jewish rites and regulations. Paul had the wisdom to see that if this were done the Church would remain a small Jewish sect. Thank God that he was able to win Peter over to his side, and therefore to win his fight. The Church ever since, however, has been struggling with those who would keep it local and parochial, rather than universal.

The third great battlefield on which St. Paul fought was that of the world. He did not hesitate to project the warfare that he experienced within his soul and within the

Church to the arena of the world itself. In other words, St. Paul confronted the world with the life and love of Christ and challenged the world to make some response. Following our Lord's example, he invaded the enemy camp and forced the issue. His demand to be taken to Rome and to be tried by Caesar was his way of tossing the Christian gauntlet at the foot of the enemy. Isn't that exactly what our Lord was doing when he entered Jerusalem on Palm Sunday? He was forcing the people to choose either for or against him. When he stood before Pilate, Pilate was forced to make a decision. Our Lord would not relieve Pilate and the authorities of their responsibility by retiring quietly to Galilee. Therefore, the Cross will forever be a symbol, not of giving up the fight and laying down the arms, but rather of carrying the fight not just to the enemy's gates, but into his very heart and mind and soul.

O God, may those who are received into the congregation of Christ's flock, and signed with the sign of the Cross, never be ashamed to confess the faith of Christ crucified; and manfully to fight under his banner against sin, the world, and the devil; and may they continue Christ's faithful soldiers and servants until their life's end. Amen.

ALL SAINTS' DAY

November 1

Who, in the multitude of thy Saints, hast compassed us about with so great a cloud of witnesses that we, rejoicing in their fellowship, may run with patience the race that is set before us, and, together with them, may receive the crown of glory that fadeth not away.

(Book of Common Prayer)

There are three major themes running through this Proper Preface of All Saints' Day like three golden threads, each of which we shall discuss in turn. The first has to do with the things we see. For instance, what does a pastor see when he looks at his congregation Sunday after Sunday? For one thing, he sees a number of faces, some of which are young and fair; others, old and tired. But is that all that he is able to see—just a number of faces? What about the joy which he knows is present in the hearts of some, especially the very young? What about the hope he knows is so strong in some of the college students as they face the years ahead? What about the love which literally fills the air when a bride and groom stand before the altar, repeating their marriage vows? What about the heroism and the sacrifice which are the daily bread of some of our older people? Experiences such as these lead us to conclude that the things we cannot see with our eyes are more important than the things we can. And this, of course, is one of the great themes of this day.

142

Referring to the great cloud of witnesses that surround us, the Preface goes on to tell us that "rejoicing in their fellowship, we may run with patience the race that is set before us." In other words, we do not have to run the race by ourselves nor on our own. Is there anything more terrible than loneliness? It is bad enough to bear when things are running smoothly. But when the race of life grows hard and steep, then to have to do it on one's own is a bitter thing indeed! That is why the Church this day asks us not only to open our eyes and behold the great company of witnesses that surround us, but also to rejoice in their fellowship, laying hold upon their sustaining strength and grace. Life does not have to be a lonely and dreary affair. It can be like one of Chaucer's Canterbury Tales if the Christian but joins ranks with the Pilgrims to Canterbury—not only with those who are stumbling along in this life, but also with the triumphant company of heavenly host who march with songs of victory and banners unfurled. We can run with patience the race that is set before us if we do not try to run it on our own, but join the company of saints and rejoice in their fellowship. That is our second great theme.

The final theme has to do with a promise. It urges us to behold the saints who surround us and to rejoice in their fellowship in order that "together with them we may receive the crown of glory that fadeth not away." The world is starving for a bit of glory—for the sight of a man who would rather die than betray a confidence or a principle. There can be no glory apart from God, for he is the King of Glory. And may I remind you that this Glory of God is not confined to his heavenly kingdom. As Francis Thompson puts it:

> The angels keep their ancient places,
> Turn but a stone and start a wing.
> 'Tis ye, 'tis your estranged faces
> That miss the many-splendored thing.[15]

And until we begin to discover something of the glory in a stone, a leaf, a shifting cloud, we cannot expect to perceive the glory of heaven. Will you not try during this season to look beyond the things you see to the beauty of the unseen, to join as pilgrims with the saints, rejoicing in their fellowship, and together with them receiving the Crown of Glory that fadeth not away?

Has anyone described more beautifully than John Milton that eternal glory which is reserved for those who love God, and which fadeth not away? In his poem "Lycidas" Milton pays this tribute to a dear friend who was drowned at sea:

> Weep no more, woeful Shepherds, weep no more,
> For Lycidas, your sorrow, is not dead,
> Sunk though he be beneath the watery floor;
> So sinks the day-star in the ocean bed,
> And yet anon repairs his drooping head,
> And tricks his beams, and with new-spangled ore,
> Flames in the forehead of the morning sky.
> So Lycidas sunk low, but mounted high,
> Through the dear might of Him that walk'd the waves,
> Where, other groves and other streams along,
> With Nectar pure his oozy Lock's he laves,
> And hears the unexpressive nuptial song,
> In the blest kingdoms meek of joy and love.
> There entertain him all the Saints above,
> In solemn troops, and sweet societies,
> That sing, and singing in their glory move,
> And wipe the tears forever from his eyes.

Almighty God, our Heavenly Father, open our eyes, we beseech thee, to behold the great cloud of witnesses who surround us, that great invisible company of heavenly hosts. Rejoicing in their companionship may we lay hold upon their sustaining strength and grace. And together with them, may we receive the crown of glory that fadeth not away. This we ask in the name of Christ, our Lord. Amen.

THE EMBER DAYS

During the Ember Season we remember, in our thoughts and prayers, the sacred Ministry. We offer our intercessions not only for those who are serving in that capacity, but also that God may "put it into the hearts of many to offer themselves for this Ministry." In this meditation we shall address ourselves to those men who are preparing for ordination. Perhaps what we say will have some relevance not only to those who are now in the Ministry, but also to those who feel themselves attracted to this vocation. We shall direct our attention to the matter of authority, for every minister, of whatever branch of Christiandom, is a person of some authority. Wherein does this authority lie? In what does it consist?

For one thing it is the authority of a duly appointed officer. Just as a country has its duly appointed ambassadors and the military its carefully selected officers, so does the Church have its duly appointed officers who are its clergy and to whom it gives specific authority. It is no fly-by-night appointment. It is the culmination of years of preparation, study, and prayer. A great many tests of all kinds—physical, mental, spiritual—have had to be met and passed. Even after years of college and seminary, there have been more examinations and usually a period of internship. The Church is very careful to surround this office with all the safeguards which the responsibility of that office requires.

The authority which is conferred at ordination is no

authority of the moment, nor is it simply local in character. For the people who are present at that particular moment are the representatives of all the people of the Church throughout the world, not only the living but those in Paradise as well. There are present, in addition to our Lord, all the apostles, prophets, and martyrs who, throughout the centuries, have poured their faith and their love into the Body of the Church. St. Paul is there with his missionary zeal, St. Francis of Assisi with his compassion and joy, the Beloved Disciple with his understanding of our Lord, and all those holy women whose devotion through the ages has contributed to the authority which every minister receives. The authority of a great tradition lies behind every minister of the Church and gives to him a dignity that is unique.

Some men are willing to rest their authority there. Because the authority of the company they represent is so great they are willing to leave it at that. They make no effort to deepen and enrich the authority of the Church by the authority of their own lives. And to these men the Gospel cries out a warning, when it holds up before them the figure of our Lord and reminds them that "he taught them as one having authority and not as the scribes." (*Mk. 1:22*) The scribes were the duly appointed officers of the religion of their day. They had behind them the authority of a great tradition, the authority of a great Church. But they had become parasites on that tradition, living off the letter of it, contributing nothing to the spirit of it.

It is not surprising, therefore, that people who wanted to know something about God, who wanted to experience the reality and the power of God, turned to our Lord rather than to the scribes, because our Lord possessed the authority of godliness. There is no greater tradition than that of the Christian Church. But woe to our people and woe to that Church if we fail to confirm the Church's authority through an absence of authority in our own lives—the authority of godliness.

There are many attributes of godliness, but there are two which are especially important as far as the Ministry is concerned, and these I shall mention only briefly. One is a thirst for truth. When one has a longing for truth, this gives to one that humility of mind and spirit which is essential to the Christian life. For one cannot long for truth without first being aware of the extent of one's ignorance—the limitations of human understanding and insight. And this leads one to open one's mind and heart and spirit to receive every new insight which might possibly come to one, often from the most unexpected sources. Revelation is not a static thing; the faith once delivered to the Saints was something new as far as the Saints were concerned, and it was delivered to them because they were receptive to its newness. A longing for truth is one of the attributes which helps to create the authority of godliness.

The second attribute is a thirst for love, which is the same thing as saying, a thirst for God. And here we see the sharp contrast between the world's concept of authority and the Christian concept. The symbol of the world's authority is the sword—a thing of physical power and force. It is persuasive, it is efficient, and its results are quick and sure. The symbol of Christian authority is the Cross whose only power is the power of its love. Its results are not quick and sure, its methods are not the most efficient, its persuasion often seems ineffective. And there is always the temptation on the part of the minister, when he becomes impatient or discouraged, to choose the way of the world rather than the way of the Cross. It is quite possible to have a parish that is crowded on Sundays, flourishing with all sorts of activities during the week, and yet is totally lacking in anything resembling Christian faith and love. As T. S. Eliot reminds us in his *Murder in the Cathedral:* ". . . the greatest treason: To do the right deed for the wrong reason."

That is why it is so important for the minister to live close to the Cross, constantly taking his bearings from the Cross, constantly testing his values by the Cross. For, "though he has the gift of prophecy and understands all mysteries and all knowledge, and though he has all faith so that he could move mountains, and has not love, he is nothing." (*I Cor. 13:2*) The authority of godliness, the authority of truth and love.

> Raise up godly men, we beseech thee, O Lord, who might be true shepherds and pastors of the flock committed to their charge. Assist us to confirm the authority of the Church through the godliness of our daily lives. We ask this in the name of Christ our Lord. Amen.

AUTHOR'S NOTE

1. T. S. Eliot, *The Complete Poems and Plays* (New York: Harcourt Brace, 1952), p. 362. Used with permission.
2. Theodore Spencer, "The World in Your Hand" in *Poems: 1940-1947* (Cambridge: Harvard University Press, 1949), p. 113. Used with permission.
3. Anne Morrow Lindberg, "Broken Shell" in *Atlantic Monthly*, January 1954, p. 64.
4. G. K. Chesterton, "The Donkey" in *Collected Poems* (New York: E. P. Dutton, 1932), p. 308. Used with permission.
5. Lizette Woodworth Reese, "Tears" in *The Pocket Book of Verse* (New York: Pocket Books, Inc., 1942), p. 329. Used with permission.
6. Charles Péguy, "A Vision of Prayer" in *God Speaks* (New York: Pantheon, 1952), p. 143. Used with permission.
7. T. S. Eliot, "Little Gidding" in *op. cit.*, p. 143.
8. Antoine de Saint-Exupéry, "Flight to Arras" in *Atlantic Monthly*, March 1942, p. 331. Used with permission.
9. William Alexander Percy, "Compensation" in *Collected Poems of William Alexander Percy* (New York: Knopf, 1943), p. 228. Used with permission.
10. *Ibid.*, "Home," p. 142.
11. *Ibid.*, "Weariness," p. 141.
12. Sören Kierkegaard, *Works of Love* (Princeton University Press, 1946), pp. 137-41. Used with permission.
13. Percy, *op. cit.*, "His Peace."
14. Elsa Barker, "The Vigil of Joseph" in *Story of Jesus in the World's Literature* (New York: Creative Age Press, 1946), p. 18. Used with permission.
15. Francis Thompson, "The Kingdom of God" in *Selected Poems of Francis Thompson* (New York: Dodd Mead, 1925), p. 132. Used with permission.